When Parents Die

Rebecca Abrams

Foreword by Dr Dora Black

First published in 1992
by Charles Letts & Co. Ltd
Letts of London House
Parkgate Road
London SW11 4NQ

ISBN 1 85238 193 0

A CIP catalogue record for this book is available from the British Library

'Letts' is a registered trademark of Charles Letts & Co. Ltd

Cover and book style design by Sotomayor Designers Ltd
Cover photography by Adri Berger

To
my father and my step-father

Contents

Acknowledgements

In the course of writing this book I have drawn on the ideas, memories, advice and support of a great many people. Some were professionals kind enough to share their knowledge with me, others were ordinary people brave enough to share their own painful memories with me. To all of them, professionals and lay people alike, I am extremely grateful as this book would not have been possible without them. Deserving of special mention are Sarah Miller for helping set up the self-help group at Cambridge that indirectly led to this book; Brenda Polan at the *Guardian* who responded to the plea for recognition of the needs of the young bereaved by printing my article; Carol Spedding at the Women's Press for taking the project seriously long before it was a serious project; Derek Nuttall, the former Director of Cruse, who gave much useful information, and Dr Gary Jackson of the Psychiatric Department at the Middlesex Hospital. Also thanks to Rabbi Jonathan Romain at Maidenhead Synagogue, the Reverend Dr Geoffrey Rowell at Keble College, Oxford, and Peter Wallis at the Oxford Quaker Centre for explaining the positions of their respective religions. I would also like to thank my editors, Cortina Butler and Penny Simpson, and my agent, Sara Menguc, for all their help and hard work on the book.

On a more personal note, many, many thanks to Jill and Jonathan Steinberg who have been marvellously supportive ever since 31 October 1981, and probably long before; to Birgitta Johannson for guiding me towards vital connections; to Cathy Troupp for *never* being bored of discussing bereavement, and to David Bodanis and Karen Jochelson for generously providing a warm, quiet room of my own in which to write the last three chapters. I am especially grateful to my mother, brothers and sisters for suffering my grief on top of their own. My deepest thanks are to my husband, Hugo, for his unceasing encouragement, understanding and love.

Foreword

The author was only 18 years old and on the brink of taking her final school exams when her father died suddenly and unexpectedly. Devastated by his death and then by the death of her step-father only two years later, she realized how few supports there were in our society for young adults whose parent dies. With the distance and maturity that came ten years later, she has succeeded in writing a lucid, moving and helpful account of her experiences and those of other young people which will be of immense help to others who find themselves bereft of a parent when they themselves are at the outset of their adult lives, champing at the bit to be allowed to be free of parental restrictions, not realizing how important still are the bonds left from childhood, until they are severed irredeemably.

For their experiences *are* special and are rarely dealt with by books on bereavement. Of particular importance for this group of young people are the ways that their sexuality is affected and the problems of being expected, if they are the eldest, to support the surviving parent and younger siblings whilst they themselves are devastated by grief. Rebecca Abrams conveys eloquently and elegantly the feelings engendered by such conflicting roles and expectations and offers helpful advice to others who may be in the same situation. She does not avoid the painful subject of self-destructive behaviours which are at their height in this age group and deals frankly with attempted suicide and anorexia nervosa, recognizing that bereavement can be the trigger that sets them off.

Grief is the price we pay for loving and if young people are not helped to resolve their grief for the loss of their very first love, a parent, their capacity to love again can take a knock which may be difficult to repair. Every young person who grieves for a dead parent will find this book speaks to them. Their surviving parent, teachers, employers, friends and relatives will also find much here which will enable them to understand and support the young adult who is bereaved. For counsellors and therapists, the freshness and honesty of this account of one girl's sorrows will illuminate their understanding of, and enhance their work with young people.

Dr Dora Black   *June 1992*
Consultant Child Psychiatrist, Royal Free Hospital, London.
Chairman of the Institute of Family Therapy, London.
Former Vice-Chairman of Cruse – the National Organization for Bereavement Care.

Introduction

This is a book for young people whose parents have died, for people trying to come to terms with death and to cope with the turmoil death has caused. I wanted to write this book because when my father and step-father died no such book existed, because there was nothing available that spoke to me about my particular loss or helped me deal with my particular grief. Reading about widows, widowers and single parents helped a little, but not much: their situation was not *my* situation; I wanted to know if what I was going through was normal. I wanted someone to show me that they understood. This book is written for people whose parents, like mine, have died long before the acceptable age of seventy or eighty; long before you are up and running with your own life; long before you are ready to live without them; whose death makes you different from everyone else of your age; makes it difficult to do things which are normal for people of your age – whose death, in short, interferes at every level with the business of being young and growing up.

In 1986 I sent an article to the *Guardian* deploring the fact that so little recognition was given to the problems of young people coping with bereavement, and calling for the establishment of a proper national network to provide the much-needed support. The article was published and soon I was receiving letters from people all over the country, agreeing, sympathizing and sharing their own experiences of isolation, depression, confusion, guilt and rage. One woman in her thirties whose mother had died when she was seventeen sent a poem written, she said, 'out of my anger, hurt and despair'. A twenty-four year old wrote: 'Your piece struck such a chord. My mother died from cancer when I was nearly nineteen. I still feel so much grief in me.' Another said, 'If only

I had been able to talk with people in a similar situation to my own, I wouldn't have felt *so* alone.' Painfully stark, these words came from a boy of nineteen: 'I lost my mother in November. I am in my first year of college and finding it extremely difficult.' They made heartbreaking reading, those letters. So many people so overlooked for so many years. Again and again they told of lack of support, confusion and solitary anguish. A student counsellor wrote to say that his ideas about bereavement had changed totally as a result of his work with young adults at Kent University:

I had assumed that such deaths involved no more – and no less – grief in someone of eighteen or so than they did with older people. I found how wrong I had been. I even came to wonder if there were not an *additional* burden of pain and guilt experienced by students, because of their separation – physical and intellectual – from their families.

I would agree with him: there *is* an additional burden for young people who are bereaved, there *are* particular problems in coping with death when you are in your teens and twenties. Death is not in the scheme of things at this time in your life. It is usually premature and unexpected. It sets you apart from your friends, interferes with activities normal to your age and stage in life, and places a burden of emotions, expectations and responsibilities on your shoulders that you are not at all ready for. Not being prepared for a death or its effect on your life makes it all the more shocking. It leaves you feeling that the whole world has become an unsafe and unreliable place in which nothing can be trusted or valued any longer.

A parent's death in your teens and early twenties creates

impossibly conflicting needs: you expect to be leaving home, moving out into the world, separating from your family, but a parent's death makes you less inclined to do those things, less confident, more inward-looking. Should you leave home or stay home? Should you care for a remaining parent and siblings, or leave them, as planned, to get on with your own life? Should you take on new challenges or shun them? You can feel left behind, but unsure how to catch up. The great rush into adulthood rarely waits for those who are grieving for a parent.

Your perspective on life is different after a parent's death and your feelings about the many changes that are taking place at this stage in your life will be radically altered too. Saying goodbye to family, friends and familiar places can arouse painful feelings of loss; it can feel an unbearable wrench, not the exciting adventure and opportunity it should be – and still is for others. Friends seldom know how to help and their ignorance can make them insensitive and incompetent. This, combined with the misconceptions of older people, whose attitude – unfairly and inappropriately – tends to be 'they're young, they'll get over it', means that young people are often left with virtually no support. Loneliness is a problem for anyone coping with bereavement, for young people it is particularly bad. Feelings of profound isolation and abandonment are often made worse by lack of formal support and recognition.

Perhaps the hardest aspect of a parent's death for young people – and the one most consistently overlooked and misunderstood – is that death, mourning and grief involve feelings of helplessness and lack of control that are exceptionally difficult to cope with when you are at precisely the stage in your life when you need to feel powerful and in control; at a time when everyone expects you to be taking charge of your life – yourself included. Immense pressures on people in their teens and early twenties often make it *impossible* to grieve. There simply is not enough time, energy or emotional strength to cope with everything. For young adults the struggle is not only how to cope with the bereavement itself, but also how to cope with it in the context of an unaccommodating world. Often the only solution, the only effective strategy for survival, is to put it off, get through the next day or week or month and deal with grieving later. Grief is delayed not because of inadequacies on the part of the individual so much as the insensitive and uncaring environment in which young adults are expected to do their grieving. But grief avoided for five, ten, twenty years becomes *more* not less difficult to feel. In other words, delayed grief often becomes denied grief, and that which cannot be expressed at the time becomes the cause of untold anguish later in life. Suppressed grief accounts for many of the problems experienced in adulthood by those bereaved in their teens and twenties. A little understanding of the mechanisms of mourning and the impact of death at this particular time in your life can go a long way to ensuring future peace of mind.

This is not a text book, it is a testimony, an account of my experience and the experiences of other people bereaved as young adults. Some of these people are now in their forties, fifties and sixties, but the impact of their parents' deaths has become no less significant in the passing years. Others are people who lost a parent in childhood but who felt the impact of their loss throughout their adolescence and twenties. Then there are the stories and experiences of those whose parents died while they were in their teens or twenties. In all cases the details have been changed to protect the identities of the many people who have so generously and honestly shared their experiences with me.

I am not an expert; personal experience of a parent's death is my only qualification. I write not as a counsellor or therapist or psychologist, but simply as someone who has also been through this particular mill. My father died when I was eighteen and my step-father when I was twenty. Their deaths were the start of a lonely, difficult time which extended into every area of my life, affecting the way I felt about family, friends, home, school, sex and work. The experience showed me how little support there was for young people struggling with a parent's death. Virtually nothing existed at that time in the way of books, groups, counselling services or – most crucial of all – understanding and recognition. Things have improved somewhat since then, but there is still woefully little understanding of the needs of teenagers and young adults when a parent dies. This book, I hope, will provide some support, show some recognition of what you are going through, and help to address the particular issues that come with this particular grief.

I do not hope to cover in this book every kind of bereavement that young people may face. On the whole I have restricted myself to addressing the experience of young people when a parent dies (although by 'parent' I mean anyone who stood as a parent in your life, be they an aunt, uncle, grandparent, godparent, sibling or friend). I have not tried to cover the needs of the person whose boyfriend is killed in a car-crash, or whose baby is still-born, or whose sister dies of cancer. These are deaths which carry their own special burden of grief and about which my own experience does not qualify me to speak. Other books exist that *do* look at these kinds of bereavement, as do organizations that can offer support specifically to people in those situations. Similarly there are books that go into far more detail than this one can about coping with problems that may be related to bereavement, such as drug abuse, eating disorders and alcoholism. The names of some of these books and organizations are given at the back of the book under *Suggested Reading* and *Useful Organizations*. Nevertheless, there will be elements common to all bereavements, just as there will be elements of your bereavement entirely unique to you. While this book is primarily written for people coping with a parent's death, it may speak to young people suffering other kinds of bereavement about how to live with sorrow and loss at an age when it is particularly hard to be dealing with such things.

. This book is about how to find a place for death in your life at an age when you are expected to be lively, optimistic, carefree; when you are expected to take risks, leave home, get jobs, be sociable, believe in the future, fall in and out of love; at an age when death makes all these 'normal' things seem very difficult, impossible even. It can leave you feeling wary, anxious, anti-social, distracted, mistrustful, pessimistic. It can make it difficult to deal with losses and failings that other people take in their stride. This book, then, is written for everyone and anyone who is feeling or has felt that impact whether or not they were first touched by death two weeks, two years or twenty years ago. It is about the experience of being bereaved when you are half-way between being a child and being an adult, when you are young and old, and when life was confusing enough already without the added complication of death. It is about making space for the vast presence of death without letting it take over your life. It is about finding ways of keeping your dead alive without having to live as if you were half-dead yourself. It is about living with death at a time when your dead should still have been living.

1   My story

*'All happy families are alike, but
an unhappy family is unhappy
after its own fashion.'*
(Tolstoy, <u>Anna Karenina</u>)

The opening sentence of Tolstoy's novel *Anna Karenina* rings unquestionably true for anyone who has experienced the death of someone they love. Every bereaved family has its own particular circumstances which make its experience of death unique. All families are complicated and death throws a spotlight on the complexities. This was one of the things I learnt after my father died: death did not tidy up things, it did not suddenly make everyone behave like angels, it just made them behave even more like themselves than usual. Death did not solve the problems, it highlighted them. Even if outwardly a family appears conventional enough, behind closed doors there is no such thing as a conventional family. All families are made up of individuals and will be themselves individual in one way or another.

It is this sense of uniqueness, of isolation that can make you feel so totally unsupported after the death of a parent. Suddenly there is a vast gulf between you and the rest of the world.

Your experience of a parent's death will be unique to you, but there will also be aspects of your grief which you share with others in a similar situation. My story, too, is unlike anyone else's, and yet it contains many moments, thoughts and feelings which other people will also have experienced. In this chapter, I tell my story so that you can see how my experience of a parent's death differs from and chimes with your own. In the rest of the book, the difficulties I and you and others face in coping with this kind of loss will be looked at more closely. For now, this is my story.

I was eighteen years old and had just got my A level results. I had done reasonably well (no As, but no Es either) and decided I would stay on at school for an extra term to have a go at the entrance exam for Cambridge. One Thursday at the end of October with a fortnight to go until the exams I was told that Cambridge wanted me to go up the next day for a pre-exam interview. Any confidence I had had disappeared completely at that moment. But in fact the interview went all right and that evening I rang my parents to tell them about it. First I rang my father. He was throwing a party for Hallowe'en and said he couldn't talk for long. He sounded very cheerful, a little drunk and as if he was enjoying himself. In the background I could hear the other guests laughing and talking. It was clear he was busy. I then rang my mother in Bristol. My parents had divorced when I was a child and both had since remarried. Afterwards I went to meet my boyfriend who was already up at Cambridge. We went back to his college and spent the evening in the bar.

The following morning we were woken at nine o'clock by one of the college porters banging on the door. He said my boyfriend had to ring home. I went back to sleep while Tim went off in search of a call box. Ten minutes later he came back saying that he'd spoken to his younger brother and in fact I was the one who had to ring home.

'Oh, it can wait. I'm sleeping.'

'No,' he said, 'it might be something important.'

'It won't be,' I said. 'It never is. You know what my family's like. It'll be something entirely *unimportant*.'

'But it *might* be, you never know. Come on, *please*.'

I did not know that Tim had already been told what had happened by his brother, but did not have the heart to tell me himself.

Eventually he cajoled me out of bed, and we set off for the phone box. It was a beautiful autumn day: clear blue sky, a light frost on the grass and the leaves of the chestnut trees burnished gold in the sunlight. I chattered away. Tim held my hand but did not speak. The phone box was occupied by a girl who was having a long conversation with her mother.

'Shall I tell her I have to make an urgent call?' I said, never very patient.

'Yes, do' said Tim, never one to make a fuss. Still I didn't think anything was wrong.

I dialled the number and my step-sister answered. She sounded dreadful, like she'd had absolutely no sleep.

'Hi, Lucy. I just got a message to ring.'

'Yes,' she said. 'Something terrible's happened. Your dad's died.' I thought she said the *cat* had died.

'Oh' I said. 'Oh dear. What happened?'

'He had a heart attack.' Lucy was very attached to the cat, I knew.

'That's awful. You poor thing . . .'

'I've been up all night ringing people,' she said.

Then I remembered the cat was female.

'Who's died?' I said.

'Your dad. Philip.'

Apparently I didn't even replace the receiver. I just let it drop and left it swinging. Tim had to put it back on the hook. I couldn't see or think; I was just crying and crying, unable to stop. Saying the only thing that was in my mind, over and over again, repeating to myself: 'It's not true. It's not happening. Not *my* Dad. It can't be true.'

I didn't know what to do or where to go. My mother and step-father were on holiday in a cottage in the Lake District with my little brother and sister. My oldest brother, Dominic, was living in Canterbury and not on the phone. My step-brother, Christian, was with his girlfriend in York. Finally I remembered family friends who lived outside Cambridge and rang them. They said to stay put and they'd come and get us right away.

While we waited, we sat in a vegetarian restaurant and had the unhealthiest thing on sale: chocolate cake. I was still crying, amazed I had so many tears in me. I can't remember if I ate the cake or not. The friends came in their car and drove us back to their house, where for the next few hours they kept us stoked up with cups of tea and allowed me to say whatever came into my head. At about four o'clock my mother rang. She had just heard the news and was driving back to Bristol immediately. At eight o'clock that night Tim and I caught a train to Bristol.

That night back home everyone gradually began to arrive from various parts of the country. All I remember is the endless cups of tea, a sea of faces and an excruciating, crushing tiredness in every fibre of my body.

The first moment when it really dawned on me that my father was dead came a couple of days later when my aunt took me with her to the florists to order flowers for the funeral. The woman behind the counter asked to whom the card should be made out and I heard my aunt reply, 'To the late Philip Abrams'.

Two days before the funeral we all took the train from Bristol to London and from there north to Durham. Arriving that evening at my father's house was a tremendous shock. I could not stop myself from expecting to see his face around every corner, to see his large bulky figure standing in the doorway, or hear his friendly tuneless whistling on the stairs. The house was so much his house, so much part of him, that it seemed impossible that he should not still be somewhere in it. Never had it felt so inhabited by him as that evening when for the first time in my life it was not. Every stroke of paint, every picture, every piece of furniture, even the *smell* of the house was Dad. The overwhelming impression of his being there was increased by the fact that my step-mother had left everything exactly as it had been. On the desk in his study there were two lists of things to do, one for that weekend, the other for the weeks leading up to Christmas. In the bedroom, the yellow jumper Dad had laid out to wear the next day was still draped over the chair. Everything spoke of his presence, but he himself was not there.

Instead there were these other people, so many of them it seemed, all talking and milling about, busy and aimless at the same time. All I wanted to do was to think about and feel for Dad; instead I was constantly obliged to be talking and sociable, to be aware of the other people and their angry outbursts, tears, and unfunny jokes.

The funeral took place the next morning in the village church. The weather was perfect, clear blue sky, frosty sunlight, golden trees, very like the day he died. As we followed the coffin through the church door, I felt more scared than anything else. My brother and aunt and step-mother had organized all the practicalities: arranged for the autopsy, coped with solicitors, settled bills, put announcements in the papers, booked the crematorium and the hearse, arranged the funeral. All I had to do was get through the interminable days. Now we had reached the church door and I was terrified.

The funeral itself was a slightly farcical affair. The coffin-bearers were colleagues of my father's and four men of less strength and more different heights you could not hope to find. Keeping the coffin on a dignified level was quite a challenge. At the little village church they misjudged the proportions of the door and dislodged the garland of freesias placed on the coffin-lid by my step-mother. Although the congregation filled every corner of the church, most of them were confirmed atheists. As if to affirm their sense of the hollow hypocrisy of religious ceremony, the vicar, who had not known my father, mispronounced his name. 'Our dear departed brother,' he intoned, 'Philip Abrahams.' A slight rustle of embarrassment ran along the pews. My brother and I looked at each other, sharing the thought that, at any moment, Dad might sit up in his coffin with a long-suffering look on his face and tell the vicar as he had had to tell so many other people in his lifetime: 'No H. A-B-R-A-M-S. No H.' For a second we were both torn between collapsing in a fit of giggles or bursting into tears.

My head was full of the strangest thoughts. I couldn't help thinking how small the coffin looked for such a big man, and wondering if they had squashed him into it. Soon after that, only moments after being so detached and clear-headed, I began to feel bewildered by it all: the people, the flowers, the situation. I started to shake violently and then could not control my tears any longer. My brother put his arm round my shoulders and held me tightly throughout the rest of the service. Beyond him there was my seventy-eight year old grandfather, looking small and sad. The day before he had said, 'If only it had been me.' I hated being stared at as we walked into the church behind the coffin; hated even more being stared at as we walked out. I felt all the watching eyes as a kind of assault, invading me when I was at my most vulnerable. More than anything I wanted to run and hide.

From the church we went to the crematorium. There was no ritual, no meaning, no time or care taken, just a clinical, utilitarian procedure, terrible piped music and the sickly warm smell of chrysanthemums. A button was pressed and a set of curtains swung down in front of the coffin. And that was it. We filed out of the building and stood for a moment on the gravelled drive, blinking in the sunshine, dazed by this brutally abrupt ending to a man's life, then everyone went back to the house and the rest of the afternoon was spent eating, drinking and talking. Some people ate too much; some people drank too much; some people talked too much. I recall wandering through the tide of bodies, not knowing where to be in the midst of this quasi-celebration. Some faces I half recognized; some were familiar but made strange by the circumstances; many were unfamiliar to me – there seemed to be so many strangers that day. All these people, and the one person I wanted to be there, not.

In the days immediately before the funeral there had been an awful, dragging aimlessness; an endless stream of neighbours, friends and relatives; a meaningless sequence of meals which we dutifully ate without appetite, and which we eventually looked forward to eating because at least food introduced some sensation into the vast numbness that had settled so smotheringly over us all. There had been so many people and so much talk, everyone offering their memories and producing a kind of cacophony of opinions about who and what my father had been, taking away the person I knew and replacing him with someone else: a husband, colleague, son. I wanted to shut out their voices and versions. By the minute Dad was becoming less and less substantial, vanishing away, until I feared there would be nothing left but other people's voices.

In the days after the funeral, however, I would sometimes forget that Dad had died, and remember instead that I had to sit my exams in less than a fortnight, and that there was an essay on Chaucer to hand in that night. Thinking about my Chaucer essay made me feel guilty, but trying to forget about it made me feel guilty too. I was obsessed with the desire to go round the house and gather up all the things Dad had ever given me and all the things I had ever given him. I wanted to take them with me. I kept thinking, 'all those books, all those records, all those pictures, letters, photographs . . .' I was terrified the whole lot would be sold or burnt or thrown away. I was worried that my step-mother might forget that I needed things, might not understand that his possessions were a part of him and that I needed anything of him I could get.

Two days after the funeral I was put on a train to Bristol. My exams were looming and I had to get back to school. It had been odd being in my father's house in Durham, expecting

8

him to be there still, but it was even odder being back in my mother's house in Bristol. Everything was so normal – that was the oddest thing of all. There we all were, having supper, going to school, going to work, watching TV – as if nothing had happened. The very normality was strange; made me feel that there was no normality anywhere any more.

For the first few weeks my mother frequently burst into tears, my step-sister was also very tearful, but I didn't cry at all and their outbursts made me uncomfortable. I simply didn't feel anything, there was no emotion. I was quite cold and dead inside. There was no sadness or pain, nothing concrete like that. Perhaps, like Eva Luna,

I did not cry, because I still did not realize the magnitude of my loss.
(*Eva Luna* by Isabelle Allende)

It worried me though: perhaps I had not loved my father? But I couldn't make myself feel what I simply did not feel, so what was I to do? Looking back on those weeks I remember how dark and gloomy everything seemed: the other people were like the shadowy figures in a dream, the rooms I moved through were grey and dingy. I had switched off my mind and my emotions, I had shut myself away inside myself.

The only clear indication that I was unhappy – and it was not clear to me at the time – was that I felt sick a lot of the time with a kind of nervous anxiety in my stomach. I didn't like this queasiness, I didn't want to know about it, I certainly didn't want to connect it with my father's death. Instead I began to overeat. It was easier to feel sick from too much food rather than from grief. Food was easier to explain to myself and to deal with: it numbed and distracted me from thinking about Dad and death, it reduced the frightening feelings inside me to a straightforward self-inflicted discomfort caused by too much bread or pudding. Without really understanding what I was doing, I was trying to replace by food all the troubling emotions I was stuffed with. And for a while it worked, but it established a new problem: the habit of avoiding difficult emotions. In many ways this avoidance tactic complicated matters, making it harder to reach my real feelings, confusing the already confusing business of my father's death with other confusing matters of diet, calories, weight. Not knowing the trouble it would cause me in the future, seeking the short-term solution for now, I got used to ignoring my feelings and denying my needs. At a time when I badly needed to be loved and to love myself, I instead devised a way of hurting myself. As if I weren't full enough of hurt already, I had to pile on more.

At home, I was irritable and bad-tempered, especially with my step-father, furious, I suppose, that he was alive at all. How dare he be alive and my dad dead. I was rude and aggressive whenever the opportunity arose, and family mealtimes were soon unbearable with me picking fights and flying into a rage at the slightest provocation. Looking back, I can see how painful that must have been for my step-father: he had looked after me since I was a little girl, undoubtedly loved me and wanted to help me, but the only part I would allow him was that of personal punch-bag. Much of the rage I directed at my step-father was, I later realized, fury with my father for having died and hurt me – and anger with myself for not having been able to prevent his death.

School was now difficult too. I had changed schools that term and had not yet made new close friends. When I came back to school after my father's funeral I felt lonely and

10

awkward. The other pupils were awkward too, embarrassed to talk to me, not knowing what to say. I could see how much trouble they were going to, to avoid any mention of fathers or death, but the harder they tried to avoid these subjects, the more inevitably they would crop up. Once-innocent phrases like 'I nearly died' and 'I'm dead tired' and 'I'm dying to . . .' had them blushing and squirming with embarrassment. Partly I felt sorry for them, but partly I was cross with them. Why should I have to deal with their feelings when they were being so hopeless in dealing with mine? Why should I have to make allowances for them, when they should have been making allowances for me?

The most baffling incident of all came on my first day back at school after the funeral in a lesson on the Romantic poets. The teacher asked me to read out a sonnet by Wordsworth called *Surprised by Joy*, a poem I did not know. I began to read aloud:

> Surprised by joy – impatient as the wind
> I turned to share the transport – Oh! with whom
> But thee, deep buried in the silent tomb . . .

With a ghastly shock I realized what the poem was about. I read on:

> That thought's return
> Was the worst pang that sorrow ever bore,
> Save one, one only, when I stood forlorn,
> Knowing my heart's best treasure was no more;
> That neither present time, nor years unborn
> Could to my sight that heavenly face restore.

When I came to the end of the poem there was a silence in

the room. I did not know where to look. Neither, it seemed, did anyone else. I did not know how many of them knew where I had been that week, what I had been doing. I did not know if the poem had shocked them too. I knew only too well, however, the feeling the poem described: that moment of wanting to tell someone something, to share an experience or thought with them, and then remembering that of course you can't because they are dead. I knew all about that shock of remembering what you had managed, amazingly, momentarily to forget. For a second I was entirely lost. Then the teacher said, 'Would you read it once more for us, please?'

Would I *what?* But what could I do? I started again, 'Surprised by joy—impatient as the wind . . .', but I was astounded by the teacher's insensitivity. What was he playing at? Had he forgotten? Had he thought it might add meaning to the lines, or enhance my reading of them? Had he intended it as a way of acknowledging what had happened to me? Or a way of forcing the others to recognize what had happened? I was too amazed to be really angry. I was almost amazed enough to think it was funny!

It took two months for the numbness that set in with my father's death to begin to wear off and for emotions to start to filter through. Three months after his death, in January, I was called back to Cambridge for another interview. It was strange to be there again: Cambridge was the city where I had been born and brought up, it was a city intimately associated for me with my father. That week I wrote in my diary:

Being here is painful and upsetting. I pass a coffee shop where we used to have milkshakes, or a sweet shop where we always stopped to buy liquorice allsorts. Everything has memories and meaning. When

12

the phone rings, I half expect it to be Dad—even in other people's houses. In the morning I hope there might be a letter in his big, loopy handwriting on the mat. I see a tall man with dark hair in the street and I half think it will be Dad.

And yet all the time I never stop telling myself 'He is dead.' I never, never forget about him or about it. It's dreadful. I have so many regrets, so many causes to feel guilty. Above all I wish he'd known how much I loved him. Why did it never seem important for him to know that when he was alive?

I feel depressed, pressurized, hassled, surrounded by pettiness, squabbling, money problems and indecision about the future. And I feel depressed about Dad.

It is as if I exist on two planes: on the surface I can think and talk about him quite calmly, and then I feel the other plane, beneath the surface one, slipping upwards. When a particular source of pressure is relieved, like after my exams or now after my interview, I can't stop the flood of despair at the thought of Dad's nothingness, my nothingness, in fact the nothingness of everything. Most of the time I seem to exist in a void of emotion, very superficial, extrovert, cold—and then suddenly I'm left stranded by a wave of feeling, shocked by how vulnerable and lonely I am.

If only someone had told me that it was normal still to feel wretched and confused several months after a parent's death. If only someone had taken time to explain that *telling* yourself a person is dead does not automatically put a stop to your hope and need that he or she is still alive. I thought I was going mad—to be so out of control of my own mind that when I knew he was dead, cremated, scattered, gone, I could still think I saw him in the street, or might receive a letter or phone call from him. The feeling of missing him, of having lost him—and a part of myself with him—were bad enough, but they were made much worse by my fear that I was going mad, cracking up

13

under the strain. Why couldn't I cope? I asked myself angrily. Why was I so feeble and weak? Two months. I should be over it by now, shouldn't I?

If only someone had bothered to tell me that there are no shoulds or oughts, that it is different for everyone, that you are allowed to feel what you feel, and when you want to feel it. That there are no rules for grieving. If only someone had said to me, 'Two months is nothing. You'll be doing well if you stop feeling upset and confused after two years.'

Two years later my step-father died. When we first heard the news, my immediate thought was 'Oh God, not again! How can we stand to go through it all again?' But I soon learned that every bereavement is unique, the death of a parent can never be prepared for. My father's death in no way made my step-father's easier to bear, because the situation, the person and therefore the grief were all entirely different.

When my father died in 1981, I was not really affected by other people's grief. I did not feel responsible for anyone but myself and I did not have to think about anyone but myself. My father and I had a difficult and unresolved relationship and his death left many tangled threads and loose ends which I had to find some way of disentangling and tying up, but it was basically just him and me to think about.

When in July 1983 my step-father died, the situation was entirely different. As well as my own feelings, this time I was very aware of how it was affecting Seth and Ellen, my half-brother and half-sister, aged nine and eleven. Most of all, I was affected by my mother's suffering. I could not bear her sorrow, but because she turned to me for help, I had to bear it. She needed me, both to help her and to help with the younger children.

When my father died, I wallowed in thinking about him and about me. When my step-father died, I was almost too busy thinking and worrying about my family to think about how I was coping with his death.

That weekend everyone was away except my mother and me. My step-father and little brother had gone up to Yorkshire to take part in a Fun Run to raise money for charity. Ellen was on a sailing holiday with a neighbour's children. My twenty year old step-sister Lucy was at a David Bowie concert in London. Chris, my twenty-two year old step-brother, was staying with his girlfriend, and my oldest brother was at his home in Canterbury.

We'd been having a lovely weekend, Mum and me, sitting in the garden, reading the newspapers, eating strawberries. It was one of those wonderful summer days when the air is busy with the quiet drone of aeroplanes and bees and distant lawn-mowers. On the Sunday after lunch we settled down on the sofa in front of the afternoon film. It was a black-and-white classic called *Mrs Miniver* and our eyes were moist with tears from the first frame. As the hero's plane nose-dived and it looked doubtful that he would return, we sat and snivelled and laughed at ourselves for being so soppy. Outside the sun blazed. The whole day was fused with a fat contentment.

Then the telephone rang.

I went to answer it and my aunt's voice said, 'Hello, love, can I speak to your mother please?' She sounded rather sombre and instead of going back to watch the film, I sat down on the stairs while my mother picked up the receiver.

There was a moment's silence while Maureen talked at the other end of the line, then my mother sat down heavily on the chair beside the phone.

'Oh God!' she gasped. 'No! What happened?'

All the warmth drained out of me and out of the day. It was as if a heavy cloud had abruptly blotted out the sun and light and warmth. Suddenly it was icy cold and very dark in the hallway. I waited on the stairs, already wanting to cry, already very frightened.

Mum hung up and came—staggered really—to sit beside me on the stairs. 'Brian's died,' she said. Her head fell forward and she started to sob noisily, without attempting to control herself. We put our arms around each other and stayed there like that, clinging on to each other, for a long time. Maybe it wasn't for very long. I couldn't tell. All sense of ordinary time had gone, along with all sense of contentment. She cried. I couldn't. Somehow her crying stopped me. Eventually her sobbing subsided and she said in a flat, exhausted voice, 'I suppose we'd better tell everyone.'

Then we began the seemingly interminable business of telephoning all the relatives and friends who needed to be told. Saying over and over again, 'I have some bad news I'm afraid. Brian's died.'

I couldn't tell if it seemed more or less real the more often I repeated those words. They came nowhere near to capturing the fact that he was dead, but somehow it was helpful and necessary to keep saying them, to keep telling people, to repeat again and again, 'He's dead.' It was a way of making it seem even a little bit real, as if by repetition we were drumming the fact into our own heads, in exactly the same way we had once learnt our times tables.

When my little sister bounded into the hall later that evening, all excited from her sailing holiday, she walked into a room full of faces and knew at once that something was terribly wrong. She says she knew from the moment I opened the front door to her and was unusually kind and gentle. When Chris and his girlfriend strolled into her house that evening, the lodger called down from the upstairs landing, 'Someone's died. I think it might be your boyfriend's father', not realizing he was standing there. Lucy was staying at a friend's flat in another part of town. No one knew the address and there was no phone. In the end we tracked her down by driving along several possible streets and asking anyone we saw if they knew her. There was something utterly terrible about destroying the contentment of each one of my brothers and sisters in turn like that. The whole thing was like a hideous dream.

The next morning, Monday, my mother caught the train to Huddersfield and returned in the evening with my little brother, Seth.

So there we all were, the summer shattered, sitting in the house, not quite knowing what to do. Not quite believing that all over again, for the second time in under two years, we were gathered together because of a fatal heart attack. How could this be happening to us? It was almost too much to bear. We'd only just got over the death of one father and now here we were grieving for the other. Just when we'd thought our lives were taking us out in different directions, here we were, dragged back to the very place and people we'd thought we were in the process of leaving.

And then there were the friends and neighbours who came and went ceaselessly, bringing food for meals we none of us felt like eating, but which we all ate anyway, not knowing what else to do with ourselves. Often these people seemed far more at home than we. They sat and talked, chatting generally or talking about Brian. I wished they would all go. I hated the house being invaded by all these people with their trite

17

comments and irritating advice. I hated the feeling that we were on display. It was all so undignified; to be a public exhibit at a time when we felt raw and exposed and vulnerable. But we had to be civil to everyone, smile and welcome them in, when what we really wanted to say was 'Oh God, can't you leave us alone?'

I can still remember the dragging tiredness which made me long for sleep but wake unrefreshed; the oppressive heaviness that descended with each morning and which sat on my shoulders throughout the day, shifting its weight every now and then in case I forgot even for a moment that it was there. I recall mealtimes as particularly awesome, each one a gruelling routine that had to be performed. None of us had the heart to eat, even if we had had the appetite for food. Mealtimes gathered us all together and made us confront the grief in each other, made us look at one another over the plates and cups and knives and forks and see the pain in one another's faces. And at mealtimes particularly it was impossible to ignore the one person who was not there.

In my diary I wrote:

The sense of general loss sometimes dims the sense of personal loss. I feel completely suspended, abject. All my personality has been wiped out by the incessant need to make meals, iron clothes. I am both mindlessly active and totally passive. I seem to be hanging, waiting, all the time, to be triggered into action by the sound of Mum crying, or the phone ringing, or the doorbell going. And to have to go through it all again so soon is awful. This time though it is worse somehow–there is no energy, no fight in me. Just a numb resignation which eats away. This time it is not my loss, it is the loss to us all which seems so cruel. I feel negated by it, wiped out, erased by the enormity of grief and pain.

18

Since the funeral the house has felt oppressive. I feel dreadful every second I am in it, and guilty and anxious every second I am out of it. And it all just goes on and on and on. There is no end to it. I see the fear in mum's eyes. The sorrow in Ell's. The silent resignation in Chris's. It is just too much. It seems no comfort that we all love each other. I come face to face wherever I look with pain and sorrow.

It has taken years and years to understand my reaction to the deaths of my father and step-father. Frequently I meet people twice or three times my age who are still struggling to understand a parent's death. One woman in her sixties told me how her father had died when she was fifteen, how she had been considered too young to understand what was going on, kept away from the funeral, not allowed to come home until it was 'all over'—allowed, in short, no room at all to express her grief. As she spoke the painful well of emotion was still there, forty-five years later, still able to bring fresh tears into her eyes. People are not computers that can be reprogrammed in a few minutes to accommodate new data. You cannot be expected to accept something so unacceptable as a parent's death within a few weeks, or easily and painlessly adapt your life to fit such massive change. It will take time to get used to an event which totally and irrevocably changes your whole life and your outlook on life. Many of the things that I experienced will be familiar to you, but there will be much else that is entirely unique to you, thoughts and feelings that you do not share even with your family. You are entitled to your own particular grief, to the uniqueness of your loss and to all the time you need to make sense of it.

19

2   First days, last rites

'I'm not afraid to die. I just don't
want to be there when it
happens.'
(Woody Allen)

In the first few days after someone has died, the problem seems exactly the opposite of Woody Allen's: the difficulty is how to keep the dead person there in some meaningful way, central to the action, involved in the ceremony, considered in the decision making.

In this chapter I hope to cover some of the ways of doing this by looking at the events that take place immediately after a parent's death and the dilemmas which you may face, such as whether or not to see the body; how to organize the funeral; what to do about memorials for and mementoes of your parent.

A great deal of responsibility falls to older children after the death of a parent, and you may now find yourself needed and expected to share the burden on your remaining parent either by looking after younger siblings or by making decisions on your parent's behalf about the funeral arrangements. These

21

extra responsibilities can be hard to handle at a time when you already have so much to cope with simply in coming to terms with the fact that your parent has died. The tension between your own personal needs and the needs of your family can cause complicated feelings of anger and guilt.

• Decisions, decisions

It seems very unfair that at a time when we are so shocked and unprepared for making important decisions we should be expected to make so many. The few days between the death and the funeral are crammed with tasks that need doing, plans that need making, choices that need taking. The additional pressure at a time which is already incredibly stressful can seem intolerable, although for some this activity may be a relief, providing a welcome distraction from the sorrow in the house, and an excuse to get out and do something.

James was twenty-one when his father died. He was pleased to have practical tasks to be getting on with, glad of the alternative to the sensation of helplessness. He welcomed the opportunity to escape the gloomy atmosphere at home, if only for an hour or two, and together with his younger brother took responsibility for arranging the post mortem (which must be done by law after an unexpected or sudden death); registering the death; putting announcements in the papers; cancelling credit cards and accounts; contacting solicitors; booking the funeral director; choosing the coffin. . . . In short he and his brother busied themselves with all the paraphernalia that accompanies a death and a funeral.

For others, however, the endless demands may be an

unwanted burden at a time when you want to be alone and quiet with your thoughts and feelings.

I remember hating the funeral director who came to our house after my step-father died and sat in the front room asking what kind of tombstone we wanted. After him came the neighbours who all had questions of their own, and then there was the vicar, asking in his mild vicar's voice whether we wanted this hymn or that hymn. I didn't want any hymns at all; I didn't want a funeral; I didn't want my step-father to be dead. I hated all these people for making us make these decisions at a time when our minds and hearts were already so overladen. Having older siblings I was not very involved in the practical tasks of arranging the funeral; my main responsibility was helping my mother decide what to wear and keeping younger siblings clothed, fed and occupied. I found this arduous enough: it was like being stuck in one of those dreams where you try to run and cannot, your limbs dragged down by some invisible and enormous force.

There is no right or wrong: what is important is to try to be as busy or as still as you personally need to be. If it is really impossible to meet your own needs because of pressure of circumstances or family demands, then try to be aware all the same of how you are feeling so that when opportunities do arise you can take them.

— Seeing the body

One of the first decisions you may have to make is whether or not to see your parent's body.

I had the option of going to see my father's body before the funeral. The idea appalled me. I was terrified. The last thing I wanted to do was go and see a dead body – particularly the dead body of my Dad. Death frightened me. It still does. The idea of seeing a dead body is still a frightening one to me.

I cannot say that I regret not seeing his body, because for me at that time it was probably the right decision to make. Recently, however, a friend's father died and she rang me one evening to ask my advice: should she see her father's body or not? She half wanted to and was half afraid to. Would it help to see him dead, would it make his death seem more real? Or would she prefer to remember him as he was when he was still alive? Would she only ever be able to imagine him as dead after seeing him like that?

Although I have never seen a dead body and had turned down the chance to see my father's body, I have since talked and listened to many people about this and my advice to my friend was to go and see her father. I told her what I have heard over and over again from other people – that it can be a relief to see the person you love. It can make the death seem more real. It can give you a few private moments in which to say goodbye, perhaps to say thank you or sorry for things done or not done. It can – many say – make you feel that the person you knew is no longer there. What you see is a body not a person. For those with religious faith or belief in the after-life, this can be tremendously comforting: a physical sign that the soul has left the body and gone elsewhere.

The other side of the coin is that, yes, it can be very upsetting. To see someone once so vibrant and full of life now lacking vitality completely can be very shocking. Some people too do not like the change in appearance that can take place – a greyness to the skin or slight discoloration. (Perhaps even just the lifelessness of the body.)

Obviously if your parent was killed in an accident of some kind or wasted by illness then the decision becomes more complicated still. Some find it comforting to recognize something of the person they knew and loved. Others will prefer to remember the person as they were in life.

For those people unfortunate enough to have to identify the body for legal reasons, there may be no comfort at all in the procedure. On the contrary, it may be harrowing, shocking, deeply disturbing. The only advice in this situation is to accept how frightened you may feel beforehand and how shocked you may feel afterwards. It is understandable that you should feel this way and it is not something to be ashamed of. Accepting your fear or distress will help to protect you a little from the additional burden of guilt and self-blame that might otherwise become a problem.

Where there *is* choice, it is important to realize that here again there is no right or wrong. It is an individual matter and ultimately at such times as these you should not do anything that makes you any more unhappy or uneasy than you already are. This is a time for doing everything within your power to help and care for yourself. Deciding whether seeing your dead parent will help or not is something that only you can do. It is irrelevant what anyone else thinks or does. You must do only what is right at this time for you. For my friend, seeing her father's body was the right thing to do. She rang afterwards to say it had been upsetting but it had also helped her. She was glad she had decided to go. For her it was the right decision. For you, it may not be.

● Organizing the funeral

The funeral is usually the main focus of attention in the days after a parent has died and will generally take place within a week of the death, although the time lapse will vary. If, for example, key relatives have to come from abroad this may mean delaying the funeral for a while. The particularly difficult circumstances of the body being missing or unidentified will also cause delay. Your family's religion will also make a difference: Jewish funerals are held between one and three days after the death with a short service, while a Catholic funeral might take place after seven days with a service lasting an hour or more.

In his excellent book, *Funerals and How to Improve Them*, Dr Tony Walter emphasizes how much choice is available when it comes to organizing a funeral: you do not have to have a religious service; you do not have to have hymns; you do not have to have a professional person to take the service; you do not have to have a religious building, a hearse or an undertaker. Legally, you do not even have to have a coffin or an official burial ground, although in practice other regulations make these last two pretty much unavoidable.

A funeral can be many things, but ideally, as Walter points out, a 'funeral must affirm both the universality and the uniqueness of death. We all die, but I die only once'. The funeral is not the be-all and end-all of mourning. A less-than-perfect funeral does not mean you will never again lead a normal life, just as a near-to-perfect funeral does not mean you will avoid any further sorrow and unhappiness. But the funeral is an important ceremony. It marks the passing of someone who has been precious to you, who has affected you, without whom you would not be as you are, and I would agree with Tony Walter that too many people put up with a ceremony that is unnecessarily unsatisfactory.

If you are in the position of having to make the funeral arrangements, some of the questions you might want to ask yourself are:

- How important is religion in your family? Is a religious ceremony appropriate for your other relatives, for the person who has died, and for yourself? If not, you might consider a Humanist service (see p. 261) as an alternative to a traditional religious service.

- Do you want to have the body prepared by a funeral director, or would members of the family like to do this?

- Do you want the coffin to be carried by undertakers, or are there relatives, friends and colleagues who would like to be pall-bearers?

- Do you want to have flowers at the service or to have money donated to a charity?

- If the funeral is going to be a large event, would you prefer to have a private funeral for close family only, followed by a separate memorial service at a later date for everyone else?

- Do you want the body to be cremated or buried? This will depend on religious belief; feelings about the existence or non-existence of an after-life; ideas about environmental responsibility. It will also depend on what you, the mourners, want to be left with after the funeral—a tombstone, a grave, or an unofficial site for the ashes which has meaning for you.

- Do you want a close friend or relative to talk at the service as well as, or instead of, the priest?

- Do you want the service to celebrate the life of the person who has died; comfort the mourners for what

27

they have lost; emphasize the hope of an after-life or resurrection; stress the communality of grief and the inevitability of death . . . It can be all or none or some of these things.

- How best to involve the person who has died? By placing a possession of theirs on the coffin; by reading a favourite poem or playing a loved piece of music? These small touches make all the difference between a personal and an impersonal funeral.

- Do you want a party afterwards? If so, do you want it at your home or at another less personal venue?

- How do you want to mark the place of burial? Do you want a tombstone or a plaque? Do you want the ashes buried or scattered? Do you want some kind of marker, such as a bench, tree or rose-bush?

Apart from these personal decisions, there are a range of legal and medical requirements. A useful guide to the procedure is published by the Consumers' Association, entitled *What to Do When Someone Dies*.

As a priest remarked to me a few weeks ago, 'Funerals are much more complicated occasions than weddings and we don't even get a chance to rehearse them!'

If you have the time and want to think in more depth about the purpose and type of funeral you want, Dr Tony Walter's book cannot be recommended too highly. He talks at length about the role of the funeral, the pros and cons of burial versus cremation, ways of making funerals right, both for the person who has died and for the people who must continue living. He makes the point that the conventional crematorium leaves the mourners totally passive—as do most conventional church services—and that an advantage of burial is that there is at least some easy form of participation. Mourners can take an active role, either by carrying the coffin or placing flowers or objects on the coffin or simply by the traditional ritual of throwing earth into the grave.

These active ways of 'helping to bury your dead' make you feel less helpless, more in control, more involved. They affirm your links with the person who has died. They also help to establish that you are still alive, active, doing things.

In other, more traditional cultures, there is not the sharp divide between the living and the dead that most of us today are obliged to accept for want of obvious alternatives. Instead, people remain very much in touch with the body of their dead loved one. Nowadays, hospitals tend to take care of dead bodies, funeral directors lay them out, prepare them and transport them, while the mourners become almost as lifeless as the dead. But in areas such as rural Greece or communities which still observe their religious traditions such as Orthodox Jews, Hindus or Muslims, the relatives and friends very much take part in preparing the body for burial or cremation. In parts of northern England, the body may still be laid out in the parlour until the funeral. In Catholic countries, devout people will sit vigil by the body of the dead person. At funerals people will touch the coffin, if not the corpse, and maybe kiss it. There is a continuing contact with the dead person.

In some parts of rural Greece the bones of the dead are dug up after a certain number of years by the next of kin. If all the flesh is gone, the bones are transferred to an ossary and the grave is then free for someone else. If not, the body is reburied and dug up again later. Morbid as this may sound to us, this custom nevertheless reveals a—quite literal—earthiness about the business of death and dying which many of us might find helpful. It allows a continuing hands-on connection with the dead person through the years when grief is still keen despite the fact that life seems to be going on normally enough without them.

— The crematorium

Modern Western culture has invented the ultimate tidier upper of death: the crematorium. A loathing of the crematorium is the one thing that seems to unite everyone who has ever been to one, regardless of their closeness to the person who has died.

> 'Someone pushed a button and off he went!'
> 'Curtains came down in front of the coffin—like a Punch and Judy Show!'
> 'The crematorium was just one big chimney!'
> 'There was awful piped music playing. I couldn't believe it!'
> 'The coffin slid away on a conveyor belt. It was really dreadful.'

Unwelcoming, functional, antiseptic places, crematoria. I have never met anyone with a good word to say about them. But unfortunately, if the body is to be cremated, there are few ways of avoiding them. Tales abound of conveyor belts getting stuck or making horrible and all too audible grating noises as the coffin trundles away. One man told me how he found himself in a queue with two other groups of mourners, all of them allocated their five minutes. Last year I went to the funeral of an old woman, which was held entirely at the crematorium chapel. The grounds were not unattractive, with hills behind and green fields and trees on either side. The

30

chapel itself was all right. But as we came out and were ushered round to the left, it was impossible to ignore the next 'party' filing in from the right.

Crematoria tend to be over-sanitized buildings, clinically tidy in procedure and place on the one hand, while on the other hand grossly insensitive to the feelings of the mourners and the significance to them of the person who has died. In trying to create places where nothing will offend, the designers of crematoria have come up with something that does nothing but offend. As Tony Walter puts it, '[A crematorium] burns bodies, but pretends not to: hypocrisy is built into the place.'

After his father's funeral – conducted mainly in a church but ending in a crematorium – Robert, who was then twenty-three, broke down and wept. It was not good hearty sorrow, but a mixture of grief and horror at the bleak and perfunctory end to his father's physical existence. Robert was appalled that a man so precious and important to him should end in such a stark, ugly building devoid of beauty and meaning.

My own memories are not much better. Above all I can remember the sickly smell of chrysanthemums — flowers I still cannot abide.

— How to make the impersonal personal

Making the impersonal occasion of a typical funeral into a meaningful, personal event is often a daunting task, and one that in the midst of intense grief and shock you may simply not feel up to. This is particularly so if the family has not been religious but still decides on a religious ceremony. Events can quickly be taken out of your hands by 'professionals' and you may end up feeling that the funeral had nothing whatsoever to do with your parent. The insincerity of the service can sometimes be extremely painful. But there are ways round the problem:

When his father died, Dan knew that they could not have a religious service. His father had been a staunch atheist and was renowned for his strident views on the matter. Instead Dan contacted the Humanist Association who were happy to help arrange a funeral that was in keeping with his father's life and character, but which still gave Dan and his family an occasion to celebrate his life and say goodbye. 'Everything was right about it,' Dan recalled, eight months later, 'even the way the tape-recorder broke down – Dad could never in his whole life work a machine.'

It can be hard to make the service meaningful for you if your parent has stipulated very precisely what he or she wants. In these situations, the person who has died can sometimes be all too present, unforgettably and occasionally destructively so.

Marion was twenty-one when her father died. In his will he had specified that he wanted absolutely no ceremony whatsoever at his funeral: no mourners, no hymns, no prayers, no music, no speeches. Marion, her mother and her younger sister had no choice in the matter if they were to respect the dead man's wishes: he had stated explicitly that he did not want a personal funeral. Marion and her family found themselves in the peculiar position of having a funeral which was in keeping with the person who had died by being totally impersonal. 'In some ways it was entirely in keeping with my father's character, since he was a card-carrying atheist and rather eccentric,' Marion says, remembering the austere crematorium funeral. 'We went in, my mother, sister and me, no one else, and we sat there for five minutes and then we left. That was it! But I don't think it helped us very much; it made it difficult to focus on what we had lost. Recently I have been thinking that I would like to have a plaque or something. Very simple, but just something to let the world know that a special and unusual person lived and has died.'

Marion's desire to have some sign that her father died is natural enough and after ten years of feeling somehow denied the significance of her loss, owing to her father's strong opinions about funerals, she is finally acting on her need for some sort of marker, recognizing that her needs are more important now than his.

Marion's situation is unusual, but it shows how important it is to recognize your needs when it comes to the funeral. As Tony Walter puts it: 'A funeral says that something significant has happened, that a human life, *this* human life, has ended.' Even when circumstances permit, few of us unfortunately will have the time, energy or inclination to start designing funerals, most of us have to make do with what is available. Nevertheless, there are various ways in which the fairly impersonal business of the conventional funeral can be made a significant event which will mark the passing of a significant person. It is possible to give most of the responsibility to the funeral director and the priest without relinquishing all hopes of individuality.

Suzanne is a journalist. Her father died of a heart attack one Sunday after they had spent the afternoon happily making marmalade together. His death came as a complete shock not only to Suzanne and her family but also to the community in which they lived. Her father had been an active member of the community and was popular and well-known. Many people turned up for the funeral who were not related to the family but were connected to the dead man by some act of kindness or generosity on his part. The risk that the funeral might have become a rather impersonal event with many people not knowing each other was avoided by the priest's address. After speaking for a few moments about Suzanne's father, he then read out the obituary that she herself had written for the local paper. It was very personal, very direct and very moving. It brought everyone's attention back to awareness of the family's sorrow and loss. It focused everyone's minds once more on the man who had died.

Neil's mother's funeral was on an entirely different scale. It was a very small affair held in the chapel of the crematorium. Only ten people attended, reflecting the rather lonely person his mother had become. She had been a religious woman but not a church-goer and the vicar was not known to the family at all. To make matters worse he bore an uncanny resemblance to Ken Dodd! The chapel itself was an ugly little building and when the sermon was over, a pair of curtains swished down in front of the coffin as if it were the end of a pantomime. The funeral however was entirely redeemed by the address which Neil had written for the vicar to read. Even the priest's buck teeth and fly-away hair could not distract from the passionate, honest and loving description of the woman now lying in the tiny coffin. It conjured up the image of someone of immense vigour, integrity, forcefulness, imagination and warmth. No one was unmoved by the celebration and the sorrow held in the words of the address. All present were for a moment able to forget the unfortunate surroundings and concentrate instead on a woman whose life was worthy of remembering and whose death was worthy of sadness.

— On the day

Even the most well-planned funeral will be upsetting on the
actual day.

I remember how agonizing I found the drive to the church
for my step-father's funeral. The funeral car drove down the
High Street so slowly, crawling past all the shops and the
mid-day shoppers in their bright summery clothes. Inside the
car we did not know quite what to say to one another; my
brother cracked a joke, I think, and we all laughed. I felt
painfully self-conscious, aware of the people on the pavement
staring in at us, but aware too how irrelevant our grief was to
them as they cheerfully set off as normal to buy apples and
bread and shampoo. Usually we too were walking down the
street at this time of day, off to the newsagent or the post office.
Inside the funeral car we were so close to the everyday, literally
a few feet away from it, but also immeasurably distant, locked
up inside this big, black car with our knees squashed against
each others'. The mixture of the mundane and the bizarre was
confusing: the funeral car and the hearse in the midst of the
lunchtime traffic and the people in their summer clothes.

Clare's mother had a Catholic funeral in Yorkshire in late
November. For Clare the most difficult part of the day was
after the service when the coffin was being lowered into the
ground. It was a freezing cold day with a biting wind, and the
graveyard had been turned to mud by the ceaseless, pouring
rain. The women had to shift their weight constantly to stop
their heels sinking into the ground. Everyone's umbrellas were
blown inside out and no one was spared the cold and the wet.
Their physical discomfort combined with the desolate, grey
graveyard and the sight of her mother's coffin being lowered

into the grave was hard for Clare at the time. Later, however, she felt that the austerity of the day was rather fitting: the elements matching her grief very well, 'as if they were angry and full of pain too', she says.

For some the hardest part of the day will be processing down the aisle with your family knowing that all eyes are on you. This feeling that your grief is exposed to the public gaze can be terribly painful. For some the shock of seeing the coffin will be the worst part. Others find they can be on automatic pilot throughout the service, it is only afterwards when they are surrounded by people at the customary funeral meal that they begin to feel unable to cope. 'I just couldn't stand it,' one seventeen year old said, 'I wanted to be alone and instead we had to have a party! I wished they'd all go home.'

The day of the funeral is painful, it is supposed to be; it is the first moment since your parent's death when you can focus fully on the fact that he or she is dead. One of the most crucial functions of the funeral is precisely this: to allow you to feel your loss and your pain. The formal emphasis of the occasion may be committing your parent to God's care; it may be to comfort the bereaved, or it may be to make some sense of death itself, but the private function of the funeral is to let you concentrate for a while on your loss. Then, having recognized that something has been lost, you can hopefully begin to find ways of living with that loss.

• Memorials and mementoes

When the funeral cannot—for whatever reason—meet all the

needs of the people involved, a memorial of some kind may provide another opportunity to do so. This might be a second service held at a later date, or it might be the planting of a tree or bush. It might on the other hand be nothing more complicated than a photograph of your parent or a piece of clothing. In the first days after a parent's death when you are desperately finding ways of both trying to keep the dead parent alive, and trying to make some sense of the death, mementoes become of enormous significance. Having something that belonged to your parent can be a kind of small personal memorial.

My step-father was a great lover of English literature. He had been the only member of his family to go to university and with his first grant cheque had bought himself a proper big dictionary. This love of literature was something he and I had shared, and it was he who taught me how to read and understand fiction and poetry. He helped me prepare for the Cambridge entrance exams and was delighted when I got a place to read English. My step-father died at the end of my first year at Cambridge; after the funeral my mother took me aside and quietly presented me with the dictionary. It is a very personal reminder of him and of my special connection with him through our shared love of books, and it is something I treasure very deeply.

Clothes, books, ornaments, a football scarf, a chair, a collection of old records, a photograph or painting. All sorts of things can be precious to you while meaningless to other people. If there is something that you think could particularly help you to feel the person you loved is not irrevocably lost to you, something that you can have and cherish because it was his or hers, then I would urge you to ask for it. Private memorials are important to all of us, not a sign of morbidity to be ashamed of.

Sometimes you may want a public memorial. This may be because a memorial service is expected, or necessary, in order to accommodate people who could not attend the funeral. It may be a way of having 'another go' at the funeral when there is more time to plan the event. It may be for entirely private reasons, or it may be a combination of these.

Joely wanted to organize a memorial service for her father. This was partly because the funeral had seemed to her inappropriate in some ways, not capturing her father's personality or achievements. The main reason, however, was that Joely's parents were divorced and her father's family had refused to let her mother attend the funeral. Joely felt very strongly that her mother should be allowed to mourn publicly the loss of her first husband and that she should be allowed to mourn publicly with her mother. Organizing the service was difficult and upsetting in many ways, but despite the problems it did take place a year after her father's death and this time Joely's mother was there beside her.

Not having her mother at the funeral had somehow denied not only her involvement and connection with her father, it also somehow denied part of herself; at a time when one part of her was so lost through her father's death, it seemed vital to have the parts of herself that resided in still-living people such as her mother affirmed. As a public event, it was not especially successful, but as a private one the memorial service was not only an opportunity for Joely to remember her father in a way that made sense, it also helped her face up to his death.

Like Marion, Joely needed to be allowed to mourn in public in a way that made sense to her. But public memorials need not

38

be services: memorials can take the shape of benches, trees, plaques or even specific actions, such as the lighting of a candle. A memorial of some kind can be particularly useful if your parent was cremated and there is no obvious sign to tell you where they are any more. Memorials are not indulgent, they are important ways of marking the significance of the person who has died, either publicly or privately.

Julie's mother was cremated when she died. The ashes were scattered in a graveyard and a rosebush was planted near the spot. Neither the rosebush nor the churchyard have any meaning for Julie and she sometimes regrets that there is no physical place where she knows her mother is. 'The odd thing is that it seems to matter more with time,' she says. 'As the awareness of Mum becomes less pressing inside me, I seem increasingly to want a firm sense of her being somewhere outside.'

Ann's father was also cremated. Her mother and older brother scattered the ashes from a mountain top in Wales, making the pilgrimage together in the memory of many walks and climbs they had made when her father was alive. Climbing this hill had been an achievement they had particularly relished. Ann had been too young to take part in these expeditions and therefore did not take part in scattering the ashes either. Ann could easily have felt excluded and been left with no clear idea of where her father now was, but after some discussion the family agreed that there was a need for a clear physical marker, and they decided to plant a tree in the botanical gardens of the town where they lived. Six months after her father's death, on a bitterly cold February day, Ann went with her mother and brother to plant a cherry tree in the gardens. Icy rain poured down and the gardens looked bleak and bare; the frail little stripling that the gardener planted seemed to capture all too well their own mood of frailty. But the idea of the blossom that would flower and the leaves that would spring from the fragile branches and the sturdy tree that it would, in time, become, was a comforting and inspiring symbol.

Trees are a wonderfully explicit symbol of the continuation of life, the process of growth and decay and regrowth, but they can of course be rather expensive. On the plus side, the cost of the tree includes the cost of tending it, which is probably comparable to the cost of upkeeping a grave or tombstone. Wardens of parks and gardens will usually be glad to oblige in helping choose a tree and a site for it, and they can also advise you as to the cost.

Benches also are a durable memorial, not indefinitely so – it depends on the type of wood used for the bench and the type of metal used for the plaque – but they are a good solid physical reminder of a person. Something about sitting on a memorial bench to a person you loved can make you feel very close to them physically.

My grandfather has a tombstone in a cemetery in north London. Several times a year my grandmother goes to visit the tombstone. Knowing where her husband is provides a real comfort. It gives him a firm place to be now he is dead which she can easily relate to. Memorials can help ease the anxiety that if you are not careful you might accidentally begin to forget the person who has died. They might just slip out of your existence now they are no longer alive. This is a problem many people share – how to keep the memory of the dead alive without having to keep all the pain of grief and loss alive too. A place where you know your parent 'is' and where you know you can go if need be, is a simple and effective way of doing that. Memorials help to keep memories alive, while allowing sorrow to subside over the years.

The final kind of memorial – for some the easiest and for others the hardest of all – is talking. Talking is a way of remembering your parent that costs nothing but the energy it takes to remember. Through talking or at least thinking about someone who has died, about the things they said or did that mattered to you, that made you happy, that hurt you, that inspired you, that annoyed you, that delighted you, you keep alive their memory. This is not the same as keeping them alive, but a way of keeping vital and relevant the parts of you that have been affected and influenced by them. This need not only be the positive things – remembering how your mother's disapproval used to hurt you can be as helpful as remembering how you loved to sit with her and chat on Sunday evenings.

Remembering good things, talking about them with friends and relatives, laughing together about the things you enjoyed and loved in the person who died, is important too. Strengthening your sense of the good things in life helps to give a little dignity when so much of the process of grieving and bereavement seems so undignified – the uncontrollable mood swings, bags under the eyes from lack of sleep, the unexpected pangs of sorrow. The person who died not only caused pain and chaos, he or she almost certainly also gave much of value and joy to your life. It is worth remembering that. It is worth being proud of that memory and keeping it alive.

In the first few days after a parent's death, you can feel as if your life is suddenly filled with unwanted responsibilities, both for other people and for yourself. Making the right decisions all the time is not possible, but having some idea of what decisions will need to be made and what the consequences of different choices will be, can help you in picking your way through the minefield of these early, and at times seemingly impossible, days. Take it easy on yourself; try not to rush into decisions that can wait for later; try not to take on more than you can manage, and do take your own needs seriously as well as trying to meet everyone else's.

3 Different deaths, different griefs

*'Death and the sun
cannot be looked at too steadily.'
(La Rochefoucauld)*

Death is always shocking, no matter how expected it is or how long it has been coming. It is impossible to live with the full awareness of death's nearness. Even when a parent's death is inevitable it is still not possible to be fully prepared for it, because in order to cope with the probability of a parent's death in the near future and yet still carry on living, we have to dull our minds and emotions to death. It would simply be too painful to bear otherwise. Even if we know with a part of our minds, we stop ourselves from knowing with many other parts. It has to be like that, it is not a form of weakness or stupidity or false optimism, it is a form of survival. As La Rochefoucauld said, death, like the sun, cannot be looked at long enough or hard enough beforehand ever to take away the shock of it when it happens. It is impossible to prepare fully for a parent's death and however a parent dies it will always be a shock.

Nevertheless, the way in which your parent dies will affect the way in which you react to the death and the way you are likely to mourn your loss.

This chapter goes through the different ways a parent may have died, including death after a period of illness, sudden death and the particularly difficult event of a death by suicide. Sometimes a parent may have 'died' for you but continued living, for example after a stroke or through chronic alcoholism, or even through divorce or separation. Each of these different deaths will lead to different kinds of grief and it may help to have some idea of what is 'normal' in your circumstances.

• Death after a long illness

When a parent dies after having been ill for some time, maybe months or years, there is more time to prepare: you can talk with your parent about how life will be after their death, and how life has been before. You can do many practical tasks and to a certain extent sort out unfinished 'emotional business' with your parent. That is the theory, anyway. In practice, the 'preparation time' that a long illness appears to provide is not always easy to use in such a positive text-book way, because it is *never* possible to prepare entirely; death cannot be totally prepared for in advance.

Jenny discovered this when her mother died of cancer. A malignant lump on one of her mother's breasts was diagnosed when Jenny was fifteen and the whole breast had to be removed.

After her mother's first operation, life at home changed

drastically and never got back to normal. Weakened by the operation and depressed by the loss of a breast, Jenny's mother became irritable, anxious and easily tired, not the calm pillar of strength she had previously been. The radiotherapy treatment also made her feel very ill and exhausted. Over Jenny and all her family hovered the constant, unspoken and unspeakable fear that the cancer might have spread. A year later, despite all their hopes that the cancer had been caught in time, investigations showed the cancer had spread and was now in her spine, liver and kidneys.

Those months, between the probability that her mother would die and the day in May when she finally did, were something close to hell for the whole family. Apart from the invisible threat of the cancer itself, there were the side effects of the chemotherapy to cope with. Jenny found the physical change in her mother extremely distressing. Listening to her mother throwing up after every meal; watching her lose her hair, lose the colour in her cheeks, lose the sparkle in her eyes, lose so much weight that eventually she was unable to sit or stand without help, unable to sleep at night and totally dependent on painkillers; watching her home fill up with ugly, frightening medical equipment, pill bottles and syringes; watching the slow, excruciating process of a life being destroyed, of a dearly loved parent being inexorably ravaged from within – these things were devastating.

How *could* Jenny get on with her daily life and see these things? It would have been like staring into the headlamps of an oncoming car. To survive herself she had no choice but to step out of the way and only glance at the headlamps occasionally. She adjusted to all the upheavals and changes to her home life, accepted the added responsibilities that fell to her because of her mother's illness. She even made herself talk about the 'cancer'. But it was still terrifying – the prospect of life without her mother. Already Jenny's mother was no longer able to do so many of the things she always had, from ironing their clothes; making meals; persuading them to do their homework or wash their hair; reminding them to clean the bath; looking after them when they were ill; offering her opinion on clothes, boyfriends, bedtimes . . . Jenny missed her already, but she shut out thoughts of how much more she would miss her in the future. Her mother was going to die, in her worst moments Jenny realized this, but she wasn't dead yet. As long as her mother was alive, Jenny held on to the small and dwindling hope that she might recover. Every remission revived that hope. Every relapse destroyed it. Life for Jenny in these two years was like suddenly being strapped onto a rollercoaster and trying vainly to carry on as normal.

In some circumstances there can be advantages to a death coming after an illness, because at least you will have had time to 'rehearse' what will happen in the future, either by discussing it with your family or simply by imagining how it will feel to come home from school or go on holidays or hear important exam results or get married without the parent you love being there. This kind of rehearsing is often extremely upsetting, but it can also be very helpful. The hospice movement has raised awareness of how useful this rehearsing can be, and hospices play a very important role in helping people who are dying and their families to discuss and come to terms with not only the death of a loved one, but also what will happen afterwards to the bereaved.

However positive you are, it is nevertheless very hard to live with someone who is dying. It is impossible to ignore not only the mortality of your parent, but also the certainty that you too are mortal and will one day die. You may also feel that to deal with this increased awareness of mortality, you have had to 'shut down' inside. You may well have experienced many of the emotions associated with bereavement *before* your parent died: anxiety, denial of their death, anger, fear. If the illness lasted a very long time, or if you have found these emotions particularly hard to tolerate, you may have become emotionally withdrawn as a way of coping with the situation–and the painful uncertainty. Emotional withdrawal can be helpful up to a point, but it can mean that once the person does die, you can be left feeling very locked up inside yourself, unable to feel anything, terrified of feeling anything because there is now so much to feel, like a great tidal wave of emotion pressed up against the dam gates. If this is so, you may need the help of a therapist or counsellor to find ways of letting your feelings out in a safe, manageable way.

You can only prepare yourself so much for death. Up to a certain point you can face the fact that someone you love dearly is going to die. Beyond that point death remains unimaginable and impossible to prepare for. It is not a shock that can be anticipated, because nothing else that you have ever experienced before is like it. You know it will be dreadful, but before it actually happens you know it with your head rather than your heart.

— How you may feel

When someone has died after an illness, the death is a double shock: there is the shock of death itself and there is also

47

the shock of finding yourself still shockable. Your feelings may well contain another shocking emotion: relief. Relief that their agony, and yours, is over. You will probably feel angry too, that your parent has caused you so much suffering and by dying has taken away any hope for an end to that suffering. The death may even feel like the cause of yet more suffering.

You may be ashamed of these feelings of anger and relief, but they are common reactions. Remember how as a small child, if you 'lost' your parent in the street or supermarket you became scared and tearful, and then when you found her or him again your reaction was not only relief, but anger too that you were made to feel afraid. It is the same when a parent dies after a long illness: the death brings your fear of loss to an end, and with the end of fear comes rage as well as relief. Perhaps the death also allows you to feel the anger and resentment that it was not possible to express while your parent was still alive, the anger which screams inside you: 'I need you! How dare you get ill! How dare you die! What about me? What about my family? How can you die like this?'.

The relief may be for yourself or it may be for your family or for the person who has died. You may have longed for your parent to hurry up and die, in which case you may now feel guilty, imagining that your thoughts somehow hastened the end. Or perhaps you feel guilty because you think now that while your parent was alive you were sometimes unappreciative.

After a parent dies there is a lot of room for remorse and guilt, a lot of room to regret the things said and not said, the things done and not done. There is a lot of scope for self-recrimination. You may blame yourself for not 'coping better' with the death when you knew it was going to happen.

You may blame yourself for not having taken the opportunity while your parent was still alive to say how much you loved him or her. You may blame yourself for your 'weakness' in being scared of what illness has done to your parent.

Jenny remembers racing down the road to a friend's house in a terrified panic one afternoon, sobbing: 'Mum's dying! Mum's dying!' The friend's mother calmed Jenny down a little and went back to the house with her. Upstairs Jenny's mother was lying in bed, screaming with pain, her face a pallid green, the skin tightly drawn across her cheek bones, eyes closed, lips drained of all colour. She was not dead, but she was dying and she was nearly unconscious with agony. For the first time Jenny was seeing all this, seeing fully the nearness and inevitability of death—and understandably enough it terrified her. After her mother's death, Jenny felt ashamed that she had not faced death with more calm and stoicism.

Paul was seventeen when his father died of cancer. Years later he still felt guilty that in the final weeks of his father's life he had avoided him, not wanting to touch or be kissed by his father. He remembered in particular one evening when he was passing the door of his father's room. As he passed his father had called out to him to come in and say goodnight. Reluctantly Paul had gone in and hovered at the foot of the bed. 'Come and kiss me goodnight,' his father had said. But Paul could not do it. He did not want to be so near to death, nor to his dying father. It frightened and revolted him. 'Goodnight,' he said from where he stood and then fled from the room.

For a long time he felt very bad about this cowardice, as he saw it, but gradually over the years Paul has learnt to be kinder to himself, more realistic about what he could and could not do at the time. Paul can now say to himself, 'Of course I was frightened. Of course I was scared to go near him. I loved him. I loved my father. But I was frightened of him—so ill and thin and about to die. Of course I was scared to go too close.'

• Death after a sudden illness

Sometimes there will be only a short illness before a parent dies. If your parent died from cancer which was not diagnosed until it was very advanced, or which progressed very rapidly after being detected you will perhaps have more in common with people whose parents have died unexpectedly (*see below*). This is also so if your parent died after a series of strokes and heart attacks, when the first one does not kill, but leaves the person severely weakened and unable to survive a recurrence. It is also the case if you have been bereaved through accidents which leave a parent fatally hurt. In these situations you will feel both the shocking impact of an unexpected death as well as the anxiety and fear of waiting for death.

When Penny was twenty-one her mother died suddenly of stomach cancer, after an illness of only two weeks. She had started to have pains in her stomach, and was taken to hospital where doctors diagnosed cancer so advanced that they sent her home for the weekend to be with her family, knowing that it would probably be her last. Penny is one of four sisters. In the last seven days of her mother's life, she, her sisters and her father kept constant vigil at her mother's bedside. It seemed to Penny like years, not days.

Watching the rapid disintegration of the person who in Penny's eyes had always seemed substantial and solid to someone shrivelled and fragile and wasted was agonizing. Watching that process take place before her horrified eyes in a matter of days was profoundly disturbing. 'I will never forget how my mother looked in the final days and hours,' she says. 'I will never erase that memory from my mind. I don't think I'll ever get over it and I'm resigned to having to live with it forever.'

The rapid progress of her mother's cancer meant that Penny had both the knowledge that death would happen and the prospect of a future without her mother, as well as the tremendous shock of the unexpectedness of this death. She had to watch the physical decay of her mother over a period of just two weeks, and grapple with the desire to hope and the realization that there was no hope. The one thing that Penny is grateful for is that the illness was sufficiently advanced and death sufficiently inevitable to stop them from 'pretending'. 'I did tell my mother the things I wanted to before she died, like that I loved her and what a wonderful mother she'd been to us. I'm glad we said those things. Perhaps if she'd been ill for longer we would never have got round to it.'

• Coping with sudden death

When a parent dies very unexpectedly, the shock is enormous. Your trust in the world is shaken; the foundations of your life are rocked. A sudden death destroys your confidence that life is as you imagine it. Time would have taught this lesson anyway; you watch news items about people killed in commuter train crashes; distant older relatives begin to die; you lose a job you thought was in the bag; a relationship comes to an end; friends move to live elsewhere . . . Over the years experience would have taught you that life is full of loss, that you do not control the world, that unexpected things will occur and will affect you. Everyone learns this gradually and often painfully, but usually it is a lesson learned over many years, not in the space of a few minutes. When you are young, you don't expect loss; you are not prepared for it. You may have relatively little experience of loss–still less of the ultimate loss of death–you expect life to be as you see it. You take the existence of so many things for granted, from the electricity that lights your bedroom without you paying for it to the parents who collect your coffee cups and pay the dinner money. Likewise you expect your parents to be *alive*.

The shock of a sudden death leaves none of these assumptions and expectations untouched. On the emotional Richter scale sudden death registers high and its reverberations are felt a long, long way from the central zone of impact.

Shirley's mother died of a heart attack when Shirley was twenty-four. They were very close and Shirley was devastated by her death. On the day of the funeral, she recalls, she could think of nothing but what she should wear. 'Several people were quite shocked, I think. They thought I was being callous, fussing about my dress, but it wasn't that, it was just a way of coping with the awfulness of it all. Fixing my mind on something at least that was still there and real.'

This kind of fixation on a seemingly irrelevant or insignificant detail is a common reaction to shock, and not an indication of lack of feeling. You might feel afraid to cross the road, anxious if relations go on holiday, hyper-aware of the possiblity of train or car crashes. These are normal preoccupations when you are trying to take on board the enormous shock of a sudden death. Shock makes people behave in very strange ways, when viewed in the cool calm light of rationality. But at the time, there is no rationality, no normality. Your body takes over, to give your mind a chance to take in this staggering information.

James had been on his way to the bank when the news arrived that his father had died. Not knowing what else to do, James continued as planned – though he cannot now remember arriving at the bank, or leaving it again.

Later on you may well find that the shock begins to wear off, and then your mind may take over again, sometimes leaving you furiously angry or frightened or depressed. These are the feelings that shock protected you from.

Jeremy, nineteen when his mother died, seemed fine at first, coping with everything, organizing everything, managing everything. It was only after a few months had passed, and his body had switched off the red alert button, that he began to feel all the emotions that until then he had held at bay. He became depressed and prone to outbursts of temper. He also started to drink heavily. Gradually he was able to connect his feelings and behaviour with his mother's death and see how the shock of her death had been so great at the time that it had inured him to the pain of grief. Now the shock had worn off, the pain was there still and had to be lived through.

My personal experience is also of totally unexpected deaths. My father died of a heart attack one night in October. I had spoken on the phone to him that evening. He had sounded happy. He had been enjoying himself. He didn't expect to die that night. He sounded like a man all set to enjoy another thirty years of life. The *last* thing he expected was to die that night.

After all, he was only forty-eight. Nevertheless, by four o'clock next morning he was dead.

My step-father died equally unexpectedly and also of a heart attack. He was taking part in a Fun Run to raise money for charity, ironically enough for a charity he had set up. He'd been training for several weeks. He'd been to the doctor for a check-up. But a few yards from the finishing line he keeled over and died from a massive coronary. He was fifty. As a young man he'd been very athletic, and although he had put on weight he walked a lot and was seldom ill: none of us expected him to die.

Perhaps for them it was the best way to die. Quickly. Cleanly. No lingering illness. No prolonged pain. My mother seemed to think so. She often said about my step-father's death: 'I'd much rather he died like that than be handicapped and stuck in a wheelchair for ten years. That would have been much worse.' But I didn't find her comments very comforting. I thought she was just trying to look on the bright side – and I certainly couldn't see it. The fact was that he was dead and even if it was good for him, it was totally awful for us. Thinking of other ways he might have died seemed pointless to me.

• Violent death

One form of bereavement which is particularly hard to come to terms with is when a parent dies not only suddenly but violently. The experience of parents of children who have been murdered shows beyond doubt the additional weight of rage, anguish and despair that accompanies this kind of loss – and as the child of a parent who has died in these circumstances your agony will be no less. Escalating terrorism, rising levels of violent crime, increasing numbers of people travelling by car, train and plane have created a lamentable rise in the number of young people left to face the consequences of a violent death in the family. Post Traumatic Stress Disorder is a term applied to the reaction of surviving victims of plane crashes, bomb attacks, fires, floods and war. It describes the wide range of symptoms suffered in the aftermath of these events, which include nightmares, panic attacks, sweating, shaking, phobias and severe depression. It is a term that applies equally to the bereaved relatives of people killed in tragic and violent ways.

One girl whose father and brother were killed in the fire at the Bradford football stadium still has nightmares years later and becomes anxious and panicky in enclosed or crowded places. Another young woman whose mother died in the Zeebrugge ferry disaster is extremely reluctant to go anywhere near water and suffers from recurring bouts of depression.

Of the various causes of violent death, murder is probably the worst of all and the hardest to come to terms with. Jake came home one day to find his father had been murdered: it was Jake who found the body. The gratuitousness and viciousness of the attack have left doubt and fear etched deeply into Jake's being. The images in his mind are hard enough to live with, but the awareness of the proximity of such violence to one's own life is extremely debilitating. How can one trust the world when such horrific things happen? How is one to believe that life is worth living? The frightful combination of suspicion, uncertainty and terror caused by this kind of death is almost unimaginable.

Two people I know whose parents died in violent circumstances—in both cases the victims of terrorist attacks, one in Northern Ireland, the other in Beirut—still bear deep

55

emotional and psychological scars; neither has recovered confidence and trust in the world, and neither lives anything like a fulfilling life, even though their respective parents died more than ten years ago. For them, the feelings of fear, anger and desolation which are normal after a parent's death, are magnified to vast and crippling proportions.

Terrible as it is, violent death need not be a permanently devastating experience for the bereaved. People do recover with time. Dr Gary Jackson, a psychiatrist at the Middlesex Hospital in London, works with people bereaved in traumatic circumstances. 'People tend to fantasize about the death,' he says. 'They wonder what the last moments were like, how terrifying it was, whether they [the victim] were in pain. Then they may feel intensely guilty about these morbid preoccupations which are in fact an important part of accepting what has happened.' There can also be an intense need to blame, in order somehow to find a reason, an explanation, for the death. This can be helpful, according to Dr Jackson, as long as it does not become a way of avoiding your own feelings of loss.

Most important of all, for anyone coping with a bereavement and especially for those whose parents have died in unnatural circumstances, is *talking*. It is, says Dr Jackson, 'the single most significant factor' in how well people adjust and recover. Richard, a twenty-one year old who came to the Stress Clinic after his brother was killed on the party boat, the *Marchioness*, which sank after colliding with another boat on the Thames, found it very consoling that other young people were in the same position and understood how he was feeling and what he was going through. 'It doesn't take away the pain,' says Jackson, 'but talking is enormously beneficial.'

The urgent need to blame, the sense of rage at the world, the lack of trust in everything around you—all these are natural reactions to a harrowing event. To lose a parent in this way is shocking beyond belief and the after-effects of such trauma are themselves shocking and painful. It is well-known that many of the children of people killed in the Nazi concentration camps in the Second World War, even though they may not have been in camps themselves, (and even though they are now adults with children of their own), have continued to suffer emotional and psychological anguish as a result of the terrible way in which their parents died.

Whether you are part of a community of sufferers, like Richard, or suffering in isolation, like Jake, makes little difference to how you come to terms with your grief. Knowing other people are in the same situation can only help if you are able to talk about your shared experience. Holocaust survivors and their children tended to avoid discussing and sharing memories of their trauma, anger and grief, wishing instead to hide from their sense of shame and guilt and escape the stigma of the past. Understandable as this reaction is, it does not in the long-term help the individual to assimilate his or her experience.

Violent deaths are extremely hard to accept and come to terms with. If you are in this position it is essential to find someone to talk to, whether a relative, a friend, a priest or a counsellor. It does not matter who you talk to, so long as you feel able to share your thoughts and feelings with that person in an uninhibited way. The advantage of a trained counsellor or therapist is that they will know how to 'hear' what you are saying, they will understand and accept, not be shocked or tell you to 'get over it'. If you can talk to someone in this way, it will gradually help you to come to terms with your experience.

— How you may feel

When a parent dies very unexpectedly it comes as a tremendous shock. You may feel very agitated and restless in the first few days. The shock and the sense of being in danger, suddenly very vulnerable, bring on a rush of adrenalin. In former times people might have needed this adrenalin for 'fight or flight', but nowadays in the days following a death, they sit around with family and friends drinking endless cups of tea, and there is nothing practical for the adrenalin racing through their systems to do. You want to *do* something, but with death there is nothing to be done. You want to run and hide, but there is nowhere to go. The thing you most want to avoid is no longer avoidable. It is a *fait accompli* and neither fight nor flight are any use to you. This useless adrenalin is why you may feel slightly sick and light-headed at first.

As the days and weeks pass you may find yourself feeling guilty: thinking that you could have done something to prevent the death, or that things you did somehow caused it. 'If only,' you say, 'If only I'd been quieter, nicer, less selfish, less difficult. If only I'd come home earlier that evening. If only I hadn't had that fight with my brother . . .' The list of 'if onlys' is endless, but usually your guilt is irrational. Ask yourself what realistically you could have done or not done, and you will probably find the answer comes back as 'not much'. It is not possible to lead your life as if people are about to die any moment, and you shouldn't now start expecting yourself to, or berating yourself for not having done so.

Sometimes after a sudden death, particularly when it is part of a larger catastrophe involving many other people, there is a powerful need to blame someone or something: the other driver; the ferry company; the doctor; the train driver . . . This need to blame can be overwhelming. Blaming someone else for this death may seem like a way of making yourself feel better, not such a helpless victim of fate. If only someone can be blamed, you think, then maybe you can make some sense of this death and make sure such a thing doesn't happen again. But it is important to understand that even where there is genuine cause for finger-pointing, the underlying need is to diminish the frightening feeling of being horribly powerless.

To protect yourself from what can become an obsessional desire to blame, you need to understand why the acute feelings of helplessness after a sudden death are so painful and bewildering. Feeling helpless threatens your fundamental sense of purpose, usefulness and significance in the world. Shakespeare puts this feeling of overwhelming meaninglessness into words in his play, *Hamlet*, when the young prince says:

> O! that this too, too solid flesh would melt,
> Thaw and resolve itself into a dew . . .
> How weary, stale, flat and unprofitable
> Seem to me all the uses of this world!

Suddenly the world seems nothing more than a 'quintessence of dust'. You find you are no more significant or powerful than a bit of rubbish in the sea, pulled back and forth and tossed about without any say in the matter. It is particularly upsetting to feel so helpless at a time in your life when you expected to be taking control of your life, not losing control.

Feeling helpless is very painful, but it doesn't last. You are not responsible for everything that happens in your life, but neither are you entirely out of control of events. Accepting that

59

you can, and could, do nothing to prevent your parent's death is vital. One of the major tasks of life, perhaps, is learning when you can take charge and when you can't. Charles Dickens' story, *A Christmas Carol*, is about a man who thinks he can control life, but who learns through a little crippled boy and a few ghostly visitors that he is not so much in control as he likes to think. And when it comes to death, he learns, he has no control whatsoever.

Feelings of helplessness can often turn to feelings of rage and you may find yourself thinking furious thoughts about your dead parent, your family, the world: How dare this happen! How dare life deal this card! How dare people die like this! How dare the world conspire to hurt me this way!

Rage and helplessness are two sides of the same coin. Rage is often the easier to bear, but perhaps the hardest thing to believe right now is that to be able to grieve you must also *allow* yourself to feel helpless. You have to stop trying to pin the blame on yourself or anyone else; you have to stop imagining you can protect yourself from ever again experiencing such pain as this; you have to feel this awful helplessness for a while, because it is only by letting go of responsibility for the event and letting go of the need to be in control, that you can begin to put death into some perspective which in turn allows you to mourn your loss and live your life.

With a sudden death, there are also likely to be lots of loose ends. Finances and personal affairs may be in considerable disorder. Both my father and step-father died intestate – without making wills. Both had a number of debts. Neither of them had life insurance or owned their own homes. Sorting these things out can often fall to you as an older child, and this can sometimes feel very burdensome at a time when perhaps you would rather be free to shut yourself away with your thoughts and sadness. It may also make you see your dead parent in a new light, and not necessarily a very nice one.

Peter was twenty-three when his father died suddenly and he had to help his mother sort through his father's affairs. Not only did Peter find considerable chaos in his father's financial business – bills long overdue, debts his mother had not known about – he also came across love letters from another woman. It seemed his father had been leading a double life for years. Peter needed to alter his view of his father as a reliable family-loving man. To discover this new man at a time when he was still deeply shaken by the sudden loss of the old one was shattering. It took a long time for Peter to adjust his view and see not only the father who had indeed been devoted and loving, but also the man who had been disorganized and dishonest. Forgiving his father for being this less likeable person was made harder because of not being able to discuss it with him. Peter felt very angry towards his father for a long time, for deceiving them all and for adding this extra hurt to the pain of his death. It was several years before he could fully accept the man his father was and accept that his love and his anger did not cancel each other out, but could exist alongside each other.

Death can also be a time of concealment as well as disclosure. Ian's mother asked him to go and collect the results of the post mortem after his father's sudden death. The report showed not only heart disease but also cirrhosis of the liver, caused by his father's heavy but largely secret drinking. In the last few years his father had gone to considerable lengths to hide his drinking from his wife. Ian had to decide whether or not it was necessary to tell his mother the full details of the report. In the end he decided not to, but making this decision meant that he had the responsibility for the undisclosed information. At twenty-one that was not a light responsibility.

• Death by suicide

Suicide is probably the most difficult of all bereavements to come to terms with. When a parent kills himself or herself it can leave you with deep feelings of rage, guilt, resentment, helplessness and inadequacy. The stigma attached to suicide makes things still more difficult as it is not so easy to talk about what happened and the sense of shame is especially painful: instead of rousing extra compassion in friends and relatives, as might be expected, the idea that something shameful and desperate has happened can, tragically, often work the other way and create a wall of silence between you and the world.

As well as the sense of shame that people bereaved by suicide often feel, the sense that something disgraceful and literally unspeakable has happened, there is also the intense guilt that comes with this kind of bereavement. You may believe that you should or could have done something to prevent the death. You may feel considerable anger towards the person who has died, towards other people for not having done more to prevent the death, and towards yourself. Perhaps the greatest problem for people trying to come to terms with this kind of death is the legacy of fear it leaves behind. There is often a deeply-held belief and fear that you too will be the victim of self-destructive impulses. It is not at all uncommon for people coping with a death by suicide to become preoccupied with suicide themselves. You may feel doomed or fated to the same end. I have heard it said of the family of a friend whose mother committed suicide: 'There is bad blood on the mother's side. She was not the first. They all have it in them.' 'It' being the capacity to take their own lives.

This kind of myth-making is dangerous and foolish and unkind. Whether it comes from you or from other people, it is immensely distressing. The particularly intense helplessness you feel after someone you love has committed suicide can make you feel as if you have no control whatsoever over yourself. Everyone has this experience to some degree after a death. It is the circumstances of a suicide and society's reaction, as well as the complicated nature of your own reaction, that gives this idea of being doomed so much force.

One man I know is still suffering – as are all his family – from his father's suicide when he was a child. The awfulness of his death, the violence and the shame of it, silenced them. What could be said about such a dreadful thing? Their shame and horror and the embarrassment of others deepened this silence until it became an impenetrable wall around each of them and between them and the world. Gary was twenty-one when he met an old friend of his father's. Until then, he had never talked to anyone about his father's death. The friend knew far more about his father and about his father's death than Gary did himself, and was pleased to share his memories with Gary. He had not even known until then how his father had killed himself, let alone where and why.

You need to know the facts after a suicide. The more information you have the less room there is for myth-making and the many problems it causes. There is enough darkness already: where you can shed light on this terrible event, it is important to do so.

63

The poet, Ann Sexton, killed herself. Years later her daughter collaborated in publishing a biography of her mother which rigorously exposed all the facts surrounding her mother's death. She was determined, it seemed, to have it all known and for there to be as little room for falsehood and fabrication as possible. Perhaps raking over the facts again and again in the course of doing the biography was a way for Sexton's daughter to come to terms with the suicide, and it must have taken considerable courage to do so, particularly under the scrutiny of a shocked and often disapproving world.

At one level suicide is an act against life and it can therefore leave you feeling you somehow were to blame. It is a rejection of life that you, the living, may feel very keenly. When a parent commits suicide, the feeling that you have been rejected by him or her is very, very painful, and it takes a tremendous amount of time and effort to be able to see that you were not a failure, that it was not your fault. It is important to realize that by the time people have reached the stage where they are able to kill themselves, they are so sunk down in their own unhappiness that the world has in some way already ceased to exist for them; paradoxically, only by being sufficiently lost to the world and unaffected by it at some level, are people able to kill themselves. Interaction with one individual is rarely enough to save a person's life when he or she is intent on taking it. It is the accumulation of many, many things, not one single event or individual that drives someone to such despair. To imagine a person you love in such distress is heart-breaking, but if possible you should not try to shoulder the entire responsibility for their despair, nor for the vast range of problems behind it.

Suicide does not always happen suddenly in a single act of

violence. Sometimes people will have repeatedly tried to kill themselves over a number of years. Sometimes people will kill themselves systematically over a period of time, as is the case for people who die from alcohol or drug abuse. If your parent died in this way the feelings you may have about the death are very much akin to those experienced by people who have been bereaved by a more 'conventional' suicide, with all the extreme complexity that involves.

Sally, now in her forties was twenty-six when her mother killed herself by jumping in front of a train in the London Underground. There was the horror of imagining what had been done to her mother physically when the train hit her. There was the horror of imagining what had been going through her mother's mind at the time. There was the anguish of the daughter whose mother not only destroyed her own life, but also through that act somehow attacked Sally's right to be alive. But although her mother's death was a shock, it was not entirely unexpected. As long as she could remember her mother had been very disturbed. She had distinct memories from childhood of her mother becoming hysterical and, finally, of the day when an ambulance arrived at the house and her mother was taken away and committed to a psychiatric hospital. She had tried to kill herself before. The difference was that this time she was successful. For Sally the damage of her mother's despair had been done before she died. Sally had been suffering since she was a child. She had felt many of the feelings that come after a suicide, while her mother was actually still alive.

Rachel's mother died from liver failure two days after Rachel's twenty-third birthday. She had been a chronic alcoholic for almost as long as Rachel could remember. It had been years since they had been able to hold a coherent conversation and in the past twelve months her mother had no longer been able to recognize her when she visited. Watching this kind of self-destruction was immensely painful. Seeing her mother drunk and often violent was terribly upsetting. Witnessing this, helpless to do anything to stop it, Rachel felt guilty, ashamed, angry, wretched – and, to protect herself, finally managed to stop feeling very much at all. When her mother finally died, it was a relief, but it also stirred up all the emotions she had protected herself from over the years. The death she had somehow to mourn was complicated; it was both a suicide and a death after a long illness. Her grief was also complicated, violent and drawn out.

• Other ways of dying

Sometimes, like Rachel, you may feel you have already lost your parent *before* the actual death. A parent may have 'died' already, for example, following a stroke or an illness such as multiple sclerosis which can change the personality completely. These changes in your parent before death may have been so great that you felt as if you had lost the person you loved months or years before the eventual 'real' death: the irritable, dependent, silent person is not the mother or father you knew. A stroke or heart attack can literally kill part of the parent you knew, making it necessary for you to get to know a very changed person. As e.e. cummings put it 'unbeing dead isn't being alive'.

In situations like these, you may have had to mourn for the loss of a parent before the death itself, and this can make it very hard to know precisely what you have lost *after* the death. You may find that you have been living in a kind of limbo which the death brings to an end and that only then may the pent-up feelings of sadness, fear, rage and guilt be released. To feel these emotions after a period of suspended animation can be a tremendous shock if you had mistakenly believed the numbness was a genuine ability to cope calmly with what was happening. When your parent dies in some sense and yet lives on in another, it can be very hard to mourn properly for what you have lost. You may feel unentitled to be sad, or you may feel relieved that your parent has died at last. In Orthodox Jewish communities this death-in-life is recognized formally: when a person narrowly escapes death, whether through illness or accident, they can if they wish change their name, i.e. they can assume a new identity and start a new life. This tradition recognizes that you cannot come that close to death and *not* lose part of yourself: when you are touched by death, a part of you dies, even if you survive.

Another way in which you can lose a parent before they have actually died is when your parents are separated or divorced. This increasingly common scenario can add significantly to the already complicated mix of emotions after a parent's death.

Gina's parents divorced when she was five, after which she spent the term times with her mother and the holidays with her father. 'I had a complicated relationship with my father,' Gina explains. 'In some ways he was a difficult man to know, and of course I didn't see that much of him. There were a lot of things left unsaid when he died, unaired grievances as well as unexpressed affection.' Gina found it hard to know where to begin mourning for her father. Anger and resentment, pain, love and sorrow all tumbled in on her in a great bewildering

67

muddle. Eventually she decided to go to a psychotherapist to try to sort out her feelings about his death. 'After a year of thinking and talking and crying I began to feel I was getting somewhere, beginning to understand what his death meant to me and how to cope with it.' What Gina also began to understand was that in many ways her father's death was just the icing on the cake. Underneath lay a whole fruit cake of feelings – equally tormented and tangled – about her parents' divorce. 'I started to realize that I had 'lost' my father long before he died. I had lost him when I was a little girl, when he was no longer there to pick me up from school, meet my teachers, watch me on sports day, admire my paintings, criticize my clothes, disapprove of my boyfriends, dig into his pocket for loose change, grumble when I came home late or congratulate me on my successes. All the normal everyday things a father is to a daughter were not part of our relationship and I had a lot of mourning to catch up on for all those things I had lost.' With the help of a therapist, Gina began to see how important it was to recognize that she had lost her father before he died, in order to understand fully the meaning of his death. The two losses had to be separated before she could fit them together again in a way that made sense.

Karen is in a similar position: her mother remarried a few years ago when Karen was sixteen and although both her parents are still alive, her mother's new husband will not let Karen see her mother at all. Their relationship has to be conducted by telephone when the step-father is out. Recently her mother invited Karen and her boyfriend to lunch. Thinking and hoping that perhaps the situation had changed, they drove over to the house, but when they got there, Karen's step-father had locked every single door in the house and was standing outside the front door waving the keys, brandishing his fist. Karen is grappling with how to grieve for her mother while her mother is still alive. She can see what she has lost and can even admit how like a death it is. 'In some ways it would be easier if she were dead,' Karen says. 'She might as well be, but she isn't. It makes it really hard. I am so angry about it – and I miss her so much. But then she's still alive, so what am I supposed to do?'

In 1990, Neti-Neti Theatre Company developed and staged a play about loss and bereavement among young people. The play is called simply *Grief* and is about the sudden death of a teenager and the effect his death has on his sister and their friends. One of the teenagers is Hazel, whose mother has walked out on the family. Eddie's death arouses Hazel's feelings of loss too.

[Dad] locked himself in the bathroom for an hour. Later he got drunk and burnt all her things. I had to grow up overnight . . . She never did come back, but we carried on. It was like a pantomime for all the family.

Later Hazel finds a photograph of her mother and brings it out at teatime. 'Where did you find that?' her father demands. Hazel replies: 'Buried in a cupboard. She's not dead, as far as I know. She was a bright, ordinary woman who'd had enough. As I remember. And I for one don't intend to forget her.' She puts the photo down in front of the mother's empty chair and says to the audience: 'Any loss is a bereavement, not just death.'

Mourning the lost parent is very difficult to do while they are still alive. If your parent is or was an alcoholic or severely depressed or dependent, you may find yourself in this position. When the parent does eventually die – which will inevitably happen sooner or later, prematurely or in ripe old age – it complicates the process of grief greatly. It is therefore vital to mourn both for the person you lost in life and for the person you have lost through death.

• Coping with guilt

However a parent died, one of the most troubling emotions the death can leave you with is guilt. Blaming yourself, regretting things you said or did, wishing you had done things differently. These are all part of the package of guilt that can land so heavily in your lap after a parent's death. What you must do with these feelings of guilt and remorse and self-recrimination is look at them and at yourself more calmly and more kindly. Hating yourself for what you did or didn't say will not help anyone. It is far better to try to understand why you behaved as you did and accept that it has happened now. It is done. Try to understand and accept rather than judge and accuse, if you possibly can.

After my father died I felt particularly guilty about the fact that I had avoided going to see him the year he died. Holidays were precious and I wanted the time to be out with my boyfriend, not bored and lonely staying with my Dad. After my father died I found a letter from him, sent a month or two before, asking me to come and spend at least a part of the summer holidays with him. 'I've only seen you for two days this year,' he had written. 'Is a week or two too much to ask?' Evidently it was, because I managed to evade the trip north to stay with him and in fact saw him only once more, for a weekend in London, before he died.

I felt guilty, awful, about that for a long time, about how I must have hurt him by not wanting to visit, not caring that I hadn't seen him all year. He must have thought I didn't love him. That was what was so terrible: he must have thought I did not love him. And now I would never be able to tell him or show him or in any way let him know. Maybe he had died thinking his only daughter did not love him. How could I live with that?

Now I try and tell myself that he was a grown man, that probably he understood that at seventeen friends seem more important than parents, that it was more fun for me being with my friends than with him. I hope he understood. It is still a matter of deep regret to me that I was not more interested in my father in those last years of his life. I would have liked to have known him a little better than I do. But I am better at telling myself that my behaviour was not so reprehensible, it was normal for a seventeen year old; that I am not to blame for his death nor the timing of it; that neither of us could have known time was so limited; that hopefully he knew I loved him.

The guilt you may feel is usually not deserved and the cause of it is not as significant as you may imagine. Your parent will have understood that you were frightened by his or her illness and impending death, and long ago forgiven a moment's irritation, a cross word, a brusque gesture, a refusal to help, a cruel phrase flung out in anger. You must forgive yourself these things too – remember how understandable in the circumstances your behaviour was; allow yourself to remember the moments when you were there, did listen, did care, did help. You are not a saint or an angel. No one in the world – except you at this moment – either expects or expected you to be.

Everyone experiences some guilt after someone they care for dies, whoever that person was and however they died. 'If only I'd been more supportive, spent more time with him,' one twenty-four year old was still saying five years later about his friend who committed suicide at university. 'Why didn't I go and see him off at the station. I didn't even kiss him goodbye,' my mother says about her husband who died of a heart attack the next day. 'Why did we have that stupid argument that morning?' a twenty-one year old, whose boyfriend was killed that afternoon in a climbing accident, asked me. 'Why didn't I go home that weekend.' 'Why didn't I write more often?' 'Why didn't I notice?' What you are asking yourself is why you are mortal. Why you aren't a superhuman being who can foresee these tragedies, predict the future and act accordingly. People often torment themselves in the months and years after a person's death with these phrases, whether that person died slowly or suddenly, calmly or violently, while asleep or in an accident. The phrases will differ with the circumstances of the death, but everyone is susceptible to feelings of guilt and blame. But feeling guilty will not do any good, least of all to yourself. You can't live your life as if it will end at lunchtime. You have to assume life will continue, that people you had breakfast with will still be alive at suppertime. You have to trust that it is safe to have misunderstandings, separations, days off and off days, time alone. You would go crazy if you had to live every second of your life as if it were the last.

But that is why death is such a shock: because you *cannot* be prepared for it and live a satisfactory life at the same time. Everyone is taken by surprise by a death: the trust that life will continue beyond lunchtime is always shattered when someone you love dies. *Everyone* is prone to re-examining the past in the light of this new, untrusting 'if only I'd known' perspective. But it is unrealistic and unkind to yourself to do so. The most important thing you can do is accept that you could *not* have known; that you are not to blame for being human.

4   # Mourning time
– the first year

*'Death produces a sudden
nothingness in the world, a hole
in the fabric of the world, with
which the survivor must learn to
live, and whether the lost one be
loved or hated makes no
difference, that learning still is
difficult.'*
(John Banville)

The prospect of the rest of your life stretching ahead
without your parent can be extremely daunting. You may
wonder how on earth you can survive these days, months and
years to come. One day you think you are coping well, the next
you feel worse than ever. Sometimes you can feel, as Dora
Carrington did after the death of her beloved Lytton Strachey,
that 'every day it gets *harder* to bear'.

Grieving is less like a smooth wide motorway than a potted,
windy, bumpy, dirt track with no lights and no signposts. Very
often you end up wondering in despair if you are on the right
road, having lost all sense of direction and distance, with no
idea how far you are from your point of departure or your
destination. At times it can be very hard to believe you are
getting anywhere, and in the time ahead there may well be
moments of real desperation. Knowing this won't prevent

these times of despair and disorientation, but the daunting prospect of a lifetime ahead without your parent can be made a little more manageable if you can anticipate some of the things that are likely to happen.

There is no foolproof timetable for mourning because everyone's reactions will be different according to their particular circumstances. But it is generally agreed that there are certain phases and stages that people tend to go through during the first few years after a bereavement. This is particularly true in the first two years. Knowing what these stages are can be a tremendous help, especially in those moments when you doubt you are recovering at all.

• It takes time

The first thing to know is that coming to terms with a parent's death takes time.

I wish someone had explained to me about time when my father died. I wish someone had thought to tell me that a month is not long enough to get used to the death of someone who has been central to your life for eighteen years. It would have helped so much to know that however normal I might *appear* after a month, a year would not be long enough to begin to *feel* normal again. I so often caught myself saying crossly: 'Come on, girl. Pull yourself together. It's a long time ago now. You can't still be feeling miserable.' But I was. Sometimes I would be cross, sometimes impatient, sometimes sorry for myself, sometimes worried that I was *never* going to feel any better. Very rarely did it occur to me that actually 'it' wasn't very long ago at all.

To lose someone you have lived with, loved with, fought with, eaten with, snuggled with for years and years, all your life in fact; whose presence is central to your experience of yourself, this takes far longer than the week between the death and the funeral.

It is ten years since my father died. Ten years last October. Sometimes that seems a long time ago. Often it seems a recent occurrence, still fresh in my memory, still quick to pull at the heart strings. People say 'once a Catholic, always a Catholic', and to that I add, 'once bereaved, always bereaved'. You do not ever 'get over' the death of a parent. A parent's death is not a fence to be climbed over or a stile to be crossed. It is an event which shapes your life from this moment on, just as, when still alive, your parent played a huge part in shaping your life. A parent's death totally alters your perspective on life. It changes the way you view friends and relatives; it alters your attitude towards work, play, sex, religion. You are not the same person after someone you love and need and care about has died, and to think of 'getting over it' is a waste of time. The very best you can hope to do – and in fact it *is* the very best you can do – is adapt, be flexible, find ways of fitting into your changed world. You do not *get over* a death, but you can *come to terms* with it. You can learn how to fit death into life somehow; how to find some place in your life for the experience that you have been through – and continue to go through.

The most helpful piece of advice I was given when Dad died was by a friend of the family whose own father had died when he was a teenager. 'Don't expect to get over this,' he said. 'You won't. You don't ever get over it. You just get used to it.' It was good advice. Not waiting for a magical day when full recovery would arrive was very important. 'Getting used to it' is a far more realistic and reachable goal. When a friend's mother died a year after my father, I passed on this advice. Later she wrote to me and said how helpful she too had found it. After all, imagine that every day for twenty years you have walked along a certain road and posted a letter at a certain letter-box. Then one day you walk along that road with your letter and find the box has gone. How long would it take to get over the absence of a mere letter-box? How much more important to you is a parent than a letter-box?

• Allow yourself to grieve

The second thing to know is that allowing yourself to grieve is vitally important. As Shakespeare put it in *Macbeth*:

> Give sorrow words; the grief that does not speak,
> Whispers the o'er fraught heart, and bids it break.

Many problems that people have later in their lives are connected with deaths not properly grieved for at the time. Frightening as the symptons of grief are, they are better than the long-term effects of suppressing your feelings.

In Jewish communities there are a series of customs which make it easier for the bereaved to mourn without embarrassment. The funeral takes place as soon as possible after the death and after the funeral the family sit *shivah* for seven days. During these official days of mourning they remain at home, receiving visitors and saying prayers. As Rabbi Jonathan Romain says in his book *Faith and Practice: a Guide to Reform Judaism Today*:

The purpose of *shivah* is to be a comfort and help to the mourners. For centuries it has succeeded in being so, and has provided a structure both for the mourners to express their grief and come to terms with their loss, and for the surrounding community to give practical and emotional support.

After the seven days of mourning come the thirty days of *sheloshim* in which mourners begin to return to their normal lives, but do not go to parties or the cinema or theatre. After that comes the rest of the first year during which the bereaved are still recognized as being vulnerable and needing to grieve. To support people during this stage, special prayers are said at the weekly service. Rabbi Romain explains that: 'The Jewish way of mourning is a series of stages, each of decreasing intensity, which accompany the mourners from the first moments of grief and gradually return them to the stream of everyday life.'

The end of the first year of life without the dead one is marked by the *Jahrzeit* or 'time of year'. This and every other anniversary of the death is marked by the mourner lighting a memorial candle in the home and saying a prayer in synagogue. As well as observing the anniversary of the person's death privately at home and publicly in synagogue, it is also quite acceptable and appropriate to visit the cemetery at regular intervals, particularly on special occasions such as high holy days, a wedding anniversary, the dead person's birthday and so on.

I describe the Jewish mourning customs in detail because Judaism is often said to be one of the most helpful religions as far as coping with bereavement is concerned. There is a lot of support from the community, and while excessive grief is not encouraged, the needs and feelings of mourners are expected and allowed, formally and informally, through specific traditions and customs and rituals, as well as through the attitude and sympathy of the community. Without this kind of recognition you may feel forced to hide your feelings, to feel guilty for still having them, to feel embarrassed about making others awkward when – so you tell yourself – it was 'so long ago'. The Jewish way of mourning shows that grief is acceptable and that grieving is an important part of coming to terms with a death.

• 'Two years is not too long'

The third thing to know is that two full years is not a long time when it comes to mourning for a parent's death.

In *Grief Counselling and Grief Therapy*, J. William Worden writes: 'Asking when mourning is finished is a little like asking how high is up? There is no ready answer . . . I would be suspicious of any full resolution that takes under a year, and, for many, two years is not too long.'

Worden's book is a textbook, written by a sensitive and intelligent counsellor, but a textbook for professionals nevertheless. I picked it up in a bookshop one day out of desperation, badly needing some information, from whatever source, about what was happening to me. Worden's cautious, measured phrase, 'For many, two years is not too long', was like a light coming back on in my head. So it was OK to feel this way twelve months after Dad's death! It was not self-indulgent. I was not cracking up. In fact I had another twelve months to go! I was normal!

When Susan, our next-door neighbour, had to go into

hospital for a hysterectomy, I remembered Worden's words again. I met her a few days before she was due to go into hospital for the operation. From the expression on her face I could see she was rather worried about it, but her words did not match her expression. 'It's nothing these days,' she said. 'The doctors are so fast. They do the operation in no time. I expect I'll be over it pretty quickly.'

Like the funeral profession, the medical profession has got so skilful and quick at its job that it is easy to forget that the time taken to complete the necessary physical task – be it disposing of a body or disposing of a womb – does not necessarily determine the time it takes to get used to being without a fundamental part of your life or your body. What the professionals do not control is how long *we* need to grow accustomed to these drastic changes in ourselves. Grieving for your parent is not unlike a period of convalescence during which you may feel weaker than usual, more vulnerable to upsets, more prone to feelings of sadness, despondency, and hopelessness.

Psychiatrists and therapists working with the bereaved reckon there are distinct stages to mourning. Elisabeth Kubler Ross, outlines five stages in her classic book *On Death and Dying*. These are:

1st stage:	Denial and isolation
2nd stage:	Anger
3rd stage:	Bargaining
4th stage:	Depression
5th stage:	Acceptance

Colin Murray Parkes in his book *Bereavement* talks about phases rather than stages and suggest these are:

1st phase:	Numbness
2nd phase:	Yearning
3rd phase:	Disorganization and despair
4th phase:	Reorganization

I offer these frameworks to mourning in case you find them useful, but there is absolutely nothing to say you won't feel anger or guilt straight away and only later experience denial and isolation. We are not machines that can be programmed: for some of us emotions will chase each other in a hectic circle; for others, one emotion will merge into another as time passes. And for others, there may be very little feeling at all for a while and then suddenly a great surge of grief. What is helpful is to have some idea of the array of feelings which may possibly crop up at some point or other and in some form or other. Then at least you can look out for them and recognize them for what they are: normal reactions to loss and normal ways of adjusting to the massive change that has taken place in your life. If you know what these feelings are and why you are feeling them, you can be less afraid of them, more patient with yourself, more able to tolerate the difficult business of grieving.

No 'timetable' for grief can be anything but a rough guideline, because there is no way of determining exactly what you will feel and when. There is a wide variation in how people mourn and not everyone will pass through each of these stages, nor in the prescribed order. It depends on all sorts of factors which will be unique to your situation. No one can determine exactly how long these stages of mourning will last. It could be anything from a few days to several weeks, it could be longer. They do not occur in neat patterns, they overlap with one another and recur at unexpected moments. Usually, with time, they disappear.

The experience of these stages and phases is *always* totally bewildering when you are the one going through them, no matter how many books and counsellors tell you they are normal, and it can be comforting at such times to know that there is an acceptable pattern to what you are thinking and feeling, however baffling it may seem to you.

Without any serious disruptions or complications during the first two years after a parent's death, you can still expect peaks and troughs in your emotions. Major events in the family, such as Christmas and birthdays, will be particularly difficult at first. By this I mean not the first few occasions, but the *first few times* each one of these occasions is gone through, and apart from these times you can expect to go through 'lows' throughout the first two years, when you may feel unexpectedly overwhelmed with sadness or despair, anger or guilt, regret or resentment. Sudden floods of tears, or a spate of bad dreams and nightmares, colds and coughs, or just feeling lethargic and restless are not unusual. All of these are a natural part of adjusting to the major change that has taken place in your life.

• Before the funeral

In the first few days after a death and before the funeral, it is quite normal to feel numb and shocked. Feeling nothing at a time when other people seem to be feeling so much can be unsettling. You may feel extremely tired, or full of nervous energy, unable to sit still or concentrate on anything for long.

You may feel like being on your own all the time or you may feel scared to be alone. In these crazy days after a death when your whole world is in turmoil anything and everything is possible. Dr Tony Walter describes this time as a limbo, and emphasizes how the word 'limbo' means chaos, a state of being between two states. This is a frightening time, a frightening place to be, unanchored, drifting, not belonging, directionless, unsure of what is real and what is imagined. Everything happening right now seems unimaginable. Walter stresses that limbo is exactly where you are: life without your parent has not yet officially begun (the funeral is part of this official transition), but neither is life with your parent officially over.

More than anything I loathed the sanctification of my father, a process that began to take place almost immediately he was dead. I knew him as bad-tempered, difficult, anti-social, allergic to physical exercise. And I knew him also as clever and sensitive and great fun and mischievous. All of these made up the father I loved. It was terrible to hear him being turned into some kind of saint. People said things that simply weren't true. It all became quite laughable at times. I listened in amazement as my father was transformed into the kindest, nicest man that ever lived. I am sure at times my jaw must have dropped in outright astonishment. It didn't help me at all, this enshrining in saintly characteristics. It merely increased the sense of unreality, the feeling that nothing was real or sure or reliable any more. And it increased my sense of profound isolation; the sensation that I was utterly alone with my loss and grief. No one understood how I felt, because no one understood what I had lost. How could they understand when clearly their memory, their experience of my father, was quite different from my own?

84

● Bad dreams and sleeplessness

You may well have vivid and often disturbing dreams in these first days after your parent's death, and in fact dreams about your parent or about death generally are a feature of grieving by no means restricted to the first days, or even the first weeks, months or years; dreams about your parent can continue all your life. But in the period immediately after the death, these dreams often come night after night and can be a source of considerable distress.

Farewell dreams are very common and can be a mixture of disturbing and comforting. Carol's father had been very ill for almost a year and had recently gone into hospital. The afternoon that he died, Carol was in her flat in London, hundreds of miles away. She had been asleep after a hard week, and in her sleep she dreamt that her father came into the room, put his arm around her and, kissing her, said 'I'm all right. You don't have to worry about me. I'm fine. I just came to say goodbye.' Carol woke up very startled and immediately rang her mother. Her mother however said nothing was wrong, but she would ring if anything happened. Within five minutes her mother had called back to say she had been contacted by the hospital and Carol's father had in fact just died. In the weeks after his death Carol felt very comforted by the dream. 'I don't know whether it was real or not,' she says, 'but it was real to me and I felt he was telling me that he was all right. The funeral was a difficult occasion, people behaved pretty badly. It was really awful, in fact, but that dream really helped.'

Sometimes 'farewell' dreams can come a long time after your parent's death. Michelle was sixteen when her father died. Almost a whole year later she dreamed that he came and sat on her bed, gave her a hug and said to her 'You've got to let go of me now. It's time to let go of me and get on with your own life.'

But dreams are not always comforting personal farewells. Jeremy was there when his father collapsed and died of a heart attack and saw in detail what this entailed. For a year after his father's death, Jeremy had terrible nightmares, waking night after night in a cold sweat, terrified to go back to sleep again. Gradually his dreams became less frequent and less distressing, but while it was going on these months of interrupted sleep were very disturbing.

Sometimes dreams are comforting, sometimes they are not, but since there are so few other ways of going over the event of a parent's death, let alone one's feelings about it, dreams are often the best way of doing so.

The week after her father died suddenly Kate, who was sixteen at the time, had a nightmarish dream that has continued to trouble her on and off for eight years. In the dream, she is in a car with her father, sitting in the back seat and looking out of the window as they drive along. Suddenly she realizes they are about to crash and knows for certain they will both be killed. She tries to call out, to scream some warning to her father, but finds she cannot speak or move. She always wakes at the same moment: just as the car crashes. Kate sometimes still has this dream, and to her dismay it has changed over the years so that it now includes other people she cares about who are still alive. Sometimes she is in the car, sometimes she is watching from the pavement; always the people in the car are close friends or relatives. 'It's as if as soon as I care about anyone, I become convinced they are going to die,' Kate says. 'The worst thing about this dream, though, is that I can't do anything to stop them being killed.'

Kate's dream reflects her anxiety about being helpless and vulnerable in the face of death, unable to protect those she loves. It expresses her horror and shock that she could not prevent her father's death, as well as her continuing fears that such a thing could happen again.

Sometimes dreams that are bewildering and upsetting immediately after the death can change over the years as your own acceptance and understanding of the death changes. Dreams can, in this way, mirror your state of mind.

After my father died I frequently dreamed that he was still alive. I didn't enjoy these dreams, I found them very upsetting, a sign that I was not 'getting over' his death, not accepting what had happened. For the first two years I was usually upset rather than comforted when I woke having dreamt about him. In one dream I was a little girl being cuddled by my father, but then in my dream my father became my boyfriend and I could no longer work out which was which. I woke very upset that I should have confused them in my mind, distressed by the sexual connotations of the dream. But probably what my dream was expressing was not some Freudian fantasy about wanting to sleep with my father, but a real enough longing for my boyfriend to be a kind of father to me. More than anything right then I needed someone to look after me and protect me. Maybe it was not so strange that I should confuse them in my mind. Even so, I felt betrayed by my own imagination; the dream seemed typical of the muddle which surrounded me outside and inside. All I wanted was peace and quiet and calm and order: *that* is my father, *this* is my boyfriend; *that* one is dead, *this* one is alive. Finito. Instead all I got was muddle – inside and out.

Later on, perhaps five or six years after his death, I had the first of a series of comforting dreams about my father. I dreamed I was at a party. It was very crowded and noisy and I was not enjoying myself at all; I felt out of place and ill at ease. Then to my surprise Dad appeared in the doorway and without saying a word he came and took me by the hand, leading me through the party to a quiet, near-empty room that I had not seen before. We sat down in a corner and spent the rest of the evening talking to one another, oblivious to anyone or anything else.

I have continued to dream about my father and my step-father for years after their deaths, and this is perhaps one of the clearest indications to me that it is totally unnatural to try to 'forget'. You simply do not forget someone who has meant a great deal to you, whether in a good sense or a bad sense, or both. A parent remains in your memories and your thoughts whether or not you are always conscious of it. It takes a long, long time to come to terms with the death of someone who has meant so much, maybe a year actively, maybe ten years slowly and quietly beneath the surface. Dreams show just how gradual this process of accepting and understanding is; like continental drift it takes place invisibly, imperceptibly, inevitably.

Dreams are an ancient and vital part of the healing process. They may be disturbing after a traumatic event like a parent's death, but they are the mind's way of thrashing out fears and anxieties that might be too much to deal with in the waking hours. If possible try not to resist dreams, let them happen as and when they will, and maybe note down what happened in the dream when you wake up. Often the events of a dream seem bizarre the next day, but a week or a month later it will be easier to see what they 'mean'.

Some people are more inclined to 'listen' to the meaning of dreams than others. If you are doubtful that dreams have meaning, fair enough, but it is worth adopting a tolerant attitude to your dreams rather than trying to prevent or avoid them, which in the long run can be destructive.

Joel, in his late teens, became so frightened of his dreams, which were disturbing and violent, that he avoided going to sleep altogether, by sitting up all night watching videos. His experience of his mother's death had been particularly frightening, and he needed to go over the events in his mind to make them familiar and less terrifying. He needed to get them out of his system. Refusing to dream and getting chronically over-tired at the same time was not helping matters.

It is natural to go over and over an event which has affected you greatly. Think how the winning goal in a football match is relived time and time again, not only in action replays and sports highlights, but in conversation and imagination after the match. That night you lie in bed recalling the line of the ball as it sailed into the net, hearing again the roar of the crowd, feeling the surge of exhilaration in your chest. Or think how you felt after making a public speech, or acting, or playing a concert. If it goes well you want to relive the moment, and if it goes badly you can't help reliving it! Think of the cliché of the mother who goes on and on about what her daughter's first child has learnt to do. Think how after a party you can't wait to phone friends or see them the next day to discuss every single aspect of it all over again.

Moments of significance in one's life call to be repeated in thoughts and words long after the event. When the events are happy or triumphant ones, this is accepted as perfectly normal: *you* might not want to watch the video of Christine and James' wedding for the tenth time, but you can understand that they do. When, however, the events are difficult, painful, frightening and tragic, you expect instead to 'get over it', 'put it out of your mind', 'get on with things'. Yet the need to relive the moment is as great, if not greater, in tragic circumstances. It is how you make the extraordinary seem real, how you give the momentous a place in your everyday life. People, you included, *need* to do this, both in joyful and in tragic situations.

Sleep can be a blessing or a curse. Sir Philip Sidney, the sixteenth-century poet, described sleep as:

> . . . the certain knot of peace,
> The baiting place of wit, the balm of woe,
> The poor man's wealth, the prisoner's release,
> Th'indifferent judge between the high and low.

But the novelist William Golding, writing in the twentieth century, said:

> Sleep is when all the unsorted stuff comes flying
> out as from a dustbin upset in a high wind.

Persistent bad dreams can make you feel that sleep is your worst enemy. If possible try to see dreams as 'useful' rather than good or bad. Try not to see it as your fault that your dreams are not sweeter – although this may be small consolation when you are actually the person who's having these frightening dreams from which you wake exhausted. Biologically sleep is necessary. Deprived of sleep we eventually go crazy and long before that we become irritable, cannot concentrate, feel nauseous and shaky. It is better to have some sleep than none at all. If you are really distressed by continually troubling dreams then it is worth going to see a counsellor, therapist or priest to work out precisely what is troubling you and how to cope with it.

Sleeping pills, tranquillizers and antidepressants should only be used with extreme caution and as a temporary measure. I was put on antidepressants for three weeks by my GP eight months after my step-father died and although I hated the sensation of being drowsy and inert, as if wrapped in a heavy blanket, nevertheless I did sleep through the night for the first time in months, and the silence in my head for a while was a relief. For someone in a thoroughly exhausted state, tranquillizers and sleeping pills may just help by allowing you to break the pattern of sleepless nights with a couple of solid ten-hour nights. For some people pills can provide a necessary bridge between the intense agitation caused by a parent's death and a slightly calmer state in which you can begin to mourn more effectively. What they cannot do is release you from the need to grieve, nor from the pain of loss.

Dreams have an important, if sometimes painful, role to play. If you didn't see how your parent died, your imagination tries to supply the information. There are so many unanswered questions, horrible possibilities and frightening ideas, yet you can't ask anyone about these things for fear of seeming macabre or morbid, so you explore these possibilities in your sleep, through dreams. Dreams allow you to continue in your imagination the relationship that death has brought prematurely to an end. Dreams are a way of supplying answers to the now unspoken questions in your head.

91

• The first six months

After the funeral everyone goes back to their normal lives and you are left to try and find some way of getting back to yours. These weeks are very difficult. Sudden swings of emotion; enormous sadness; sleeplessness; confusion, all are feelings to be expected at this time. Usually support from close friends and relatives continues for a little while, but not nearly long enough. For the many people who no longer belong to traditional religious communities, there is not much in the way of formal structures for supporting the bereaved. Instead, not knowing what else to do, and thinking it is best to be busy, most people tend to go back to school or university or work within a few days of the funeral.

Perhaps you are frightened of what will happen if you leave yourself time to think and feel. Perhaps other people are telling you that keeping busy is the best thing to do. Perhaps you want to do something to fill the yawning gap left by your parent's death.

Unfortunately the return to school, college or work can be very hard. Often it throws you into a situation where very few people know what has happened to you or make allowances for you. The pressure to cover your feelings, avoid embarrassing shows of emotion, and appear as normal as possible is very strong. But very likely you will be feeling far from normal, often far *more* touched by death than before.

When I went back to college after my step-father's death I felt as if I had some kind of disease and that other people could see it just from looking at me. I imagined they were afraid of being contaminated by this death that had so afflicted me. Surrounded by college friends, I felt incredibly lonely, shut inside a glass bubble, unable to reach the world and unable to be reached by it.

Other people's awkwardness and embarrassment can be very hurtful. Hugh was working as a young student teacher when his father died. He went back to work after the funeral and found it a most wounding experience. No one said anything at all about his father's death. 'There was only one other teacher who spoke to me and even he was too embarrassed to ask directly how I was, but he did ask how my mother was doing. He kept asking after her, even several months later. It was an indirect way of showing concern for me and I really appreciated it. It made a lot of difference.'

At school you have to cope with other people's embarrassment; you have to cope with exams and homework; you have to put up with the dramas of friends, which in comparison to the death of a parent may seem pathetically trivial. Even your closest friends can run out of sympathy surprisingly quickly.

At work you try to appear normal when in fact you are feeling strange and unlike yourself. You have to rise to challenges that you may not feel up to yet. It is not unusual, after a major bereavement, to feel withdrawn, easily tired, lacking in energy and confidence, especially if you are distracted by worries about your family. If it is your first job and important to you to do well, this can be another source of pressure.

It can be hard to say to teachers or employers 'Give me a break. This is a hard time for me.' You feel you are making excuses and may be worried that they will think so too.

93

Particularly when you are young, it seems that the world does not think frailty of any kind is acceptable. Society demands from the young unflagging energy, drive, commitment, enthusiasm and confidence. It is not very tolerant of the effects of bereavement.

I was being interviewed for a job by the BBC once, a year or two after my father's death, and the interviewer kept badgering me to explain why I hadn't watched Breakfast TV when it first started. He thought it showed a lack of interest. I thought he should have read my CV more carefully. When he asked for the third time why I had nothing to say about breakfast television, I snapped back, 'Because it coincided with my father dying and I had rather more important things to think about!' I didn't get the job, but I was glad I'd spoken up. I really had nothing to say about the launch of breakfast television. It belonged to a phase of my life which was still only a haze of unhappiness.

Having your experience denied and being made to feel somehow invisible does not help you settle back into school or work. It hurts to be made to feel like a social pariah, the person no one wants to have around, the misery-guts, the harbinger of doom and gloom. When I went back to school after my father died I found it very upsetting that no one actually came out with it and asked how I was, neither teachers nor pupils. No one mentioned that I had been off school for a week. Some people clearly avoided me, and if that was not possible, evaded any form of conversation that might bring up the dreaded topic of death.

In these situations where people seem intent on avoiding all mention of what has happened, or perhaps genuinely do not know what has happened, it is worth telling certain people who

94

need to know, such as bosses, tutors, headmasters. It is important that they can take into account the fact that you are reeling from a parent's death when it comes to assessing your behaviour – as they have to do. If they do not know the circumstances, it is hard for them to understand why you cannot do your homework or are not meeting deadlines; that you are feeling miserable and your concentration is nowhere; that you can't sleep at night for bad dreams; that the rest of the family is in a similar state of disarray; that you may be moving from the home where you have lived all your life; that your mother has had to go out to work to make up the shortfall in the family income, and that you now have to shop on the way home from school and make supper every night, and afterwards are simply too tired to do your homework. It may not turn teachers, tutors or employers into sensitive, caring, tolerant people, but it may – and anything that helps you right now is worth a try.

This is the time when you may feel very out of sync with other members of your family – either because they still seem stuck in a more intense state of grief than you, or because they seem to be coping much better than you.

One nineteen year old was infuriated by her mother's refusal to throw out any of her dead father's clothes. She wanted to get them out of the house; only then would she really be able to get on with her life again. But her mother was not ready; it made her feel safe having her husband's clothes around, as if a bit of him was still with her. Her justification that it would somehow be disrespectful to get rid of the clothes 'so soon' exasperated and distressed her daughter, who found the sight of her dead father's suits hanging in the cupboard morbid, not comforting.

Different ways of expressing grief can cause conflict too: Hattie's mother and younger sister talked and cried openly, which she found hard to handle. Hattie, who was sixteen, wanted only to be left alone with her thoughts and feelings. She didn't want to join in these emotional displays which she found self-indulgent. She was irritated and revolted by what was for them very helpful.

This is a time when you may well feel fine for a day or two, and then just when you think you are 'over it' you crash, and find yourself feeling more wretched than you did before. Each time you think you're over the worst, another wave of sorrow engulfs you, more powerfully than the last. In his account of his wife's death and its aftermath, *A Grief Observed*, C. S. Lewis describes these sudden pangs of grief:

> There comes a sudden jab of red-hot memory and all this 'commonsense' vanishes like an ant in the mouth of a furnace.

It is a profoundly distressing period, when your feelings are somehow not your own, and there are very few guidelines or supports. How normal should you be? How happy is it OK to be? How unhappy is it OK to be? Can you talk about your father or mother? Should you be spending more time at home?

In these first months you can often feel torn between wanting life to resume as quickly as possible, wanting to stop thinking about death and pain and loss and, on the other hand, wanting to keep the dead person alive in some way – through talking about them, mentioning their name, thinking about them, wearing their clothes. These two desires – to remember and to forget – can exist at the same time.

Helen, whose mother died when she was seventeen, could not bear to be at home where everything was so gloomy and morbid, but every time she went out with her friends felt guilty. She felt she ought not to be having a good time, felt guilty for trying to forget. She needed friends to make her feel more normal, but felt wrong for appearing to 'recover' so quickly after her mother's death.

I remember similar feelings: being completely fed up with being different from my friends, but somehow not really quite being able to enjoy doing the things they were doing. After one party the gap between the fun everyone else seemed to be having and the fun I was trying and failing to have was too much: I broke down in tears, to the bewilderment of friends, and just howled for about an hour. Everything looked so black. I didn't want to be bereaved, I wanted to be like everyone else; I wanted to forget about death and grief and pain, but it seemed impossible.

You may find yourself afraid that you will forget your parent, as scared of getting better as you are of not getting better. I was torn between wanting to forget what had happened and being scared of forgetting.

This fear of forgetting is unfounded: there is no chance that you will forget. The memory of a person is not like a photograph that fades with time, despite your fears. Your anxiety that you will lose the dead person utterly if you forget them for a moment is also baseless. There is no harm in trying to forget from time to time. It is not wrong to smile, laugh, have fun and enjoy yourself after someone has died. Constant unrelieved feelings of anxiety, fear and pain lead eventually to serious depression and ultimately to complete break down. You need to have moments off from grief – if only to recharge your batteries for coping with the next bout of sorrow. Often enough, it will not seem possible to find enjoyment in life, so when the opportunity arises to feel OK for a while, don't feel guilty about it, be grateful for it. It is not wrong, it is absolutely essential; you need these moments of respite: even a screaming child is silent in the moments when it is drawing breath.

There are no rules. The only guideline is that if the first week before the funeral is a phase of limbo-chaos, this is a phase of active-turmoil, a phase of mirrors and mirages, where nothing is as it seems, nothing feels solid or reliable. All you can do is stick with it and try and trust that you will come out the other side eventually into a more substantial world.

• Six months to a year

You must still expect to feel considerable grief six months after a parent's death. Your moods will continue to be unpredictable. 'Red-hot memory' can still play havoc with your emotions, and you may well find that only now is the fact of your parent's death and its implications for the rest of your life beginning to sink in. Depression and anger about a parent's death are often slow to emerge and it is now, seven or eight months later when you expect to be 'better', that you instead feel particularly vulnerable and unhappy.

After my father's funeral was over I did not cry again for six months, and it was closer to eight months before I could really look at his death straight on and face what it meant. Until then I was on hold, pretty miserable, just about coping, but not really getting anywhere in terms of making some sense of his death and what it meant for me.

It took eight months for me to discover, as many others have, that depression is one aspect of mourning that tends to appear later rather than sooner. Just when I thought things were beginning to settle down, after the initial shock had worn off and the anger had subsided and the acute pain of missing my father had lessened, it was only *then* that I found myself struggling with thick, heavy, deadening despair.

This delayed reaction is in part a mechanism to protect you from the full impact of a death until you are ready to cope with it. You need a great deal of energy and emotional reserves simply to keep going in the first six months; some things have to wait for a while.

My father's death coincided with my year off before going to university. A few months after he died, I set off as planned to work on a campsite in France. There was a lot to cope with: I had left home for the first time; I was without my friends, my family and my belongings for the first time; I was in a new place, doing a new job, living with new people. To begin with, I was simply too busy to have time to grieve. It wasn't until life settled down on the campsite that my feelings began to emerge. With the routine life, the quiet afternoons and the distance from people I knew and cared about, it became possible to think about what had happened – and begin to feel it too. But it came as a shock to be feeling these things so long after the event. I thought I'd already had my period of despair and loneliness and confusion. I thought it would be a gradual return to normality from Month Three onwards.

There was the same time-lag after my step-father's death. It was nine months later and I was writing in my diary:

Yet another day spent wandering around in tears. When is this depression going to lift? It is so exhausting this feeling of lethargic misery. I feel isolated and lonely the whole time. I still haven't accepted that he is dead. I still imagine he is alive. I hate him and Dad for having died. Five days in every seven I am depressed. I feel lonely and miserable and depressed.

Grief, as I found out, has its own timing and is not averse to going back and doing certain things again. Grief does not have some checklist of stages which are gone through in sequence and neatly ticked off. It has a maze which it builds as it goes along, blocking off an entrance here, making an exit there, darting back on itself, advancing in mysterious, twisting routes which rarely feel like an advance to those stuck in it. Professionals may pick out clear patterns, but they are hovering overhead in helicopters and their perspective is different. For those in the maze no pattern is usually visible.

What's more, you can feel very alone in the maze at this stage. People you had relied on in the early days to give support may well be withdrawing into themselves to try to cope with their own loss. Friends can find it hard to remember that seven or eight months, which seems a long time to them, is no time at all for you.

After Maureen's mother died, Maureen had to go up to Edinburgh to start her first year as an undergraduate. She was determined to cope, determined to keep up appearances of being just like all the other students. 'In the end,' she says, 'I made myself ill with the effort of pretending.' At the end of her first year she dropped out and came back to London. Her friends were little help. 'They couldn't understand what I was going through. And because I had had rather a difficult relationship with my mother and always complained about her, some of them even said to me, 'But you didn't like your mother, did you? Why are you so upset?' They really couldn't see. I used to feel very angry with them for not understanding. And of course they expected me to be over it in a week.'

The only person whom Maureen did feel at ease with was a girl she didn't know that well, but whose own mother had died not long before. They rarely spoke explicitly about what they were thinking and feeling, 'but I knew she basically understood what it was like. We just used to sit in silence a lot of the time, but it was better than being with other friends who expected me to be just like them.'

The fact that friends have seldom been through a bereavement means they simply cannot know how long grief lasts, and inevitably this can leave you feeling very isolated and abandoned. You can also feel envious of other people for *not* knowing what you are going through, envious of the fact that they are not going through it themselves. I would find myself thinking, 'Why me? Why do I have to be the one with a dead father?' Or else I would think, 'You wait! It'll happen to you too one day.' Being with friends and their parents at cheerful family occasions sometimes felt comforting, but more often it left me feeling an outsider, very lonely, and envious of their complacent enjoyment of one another.

Sometimes friends will have complicated reasons of their own for failing to be as supportive as you need them to be. One girl whom I'd considered a very close friend until the death of my step-father proved unable to empathize with or tolerate the way that his death affected me. Six months after his death I was in a terrible state and very miserable – but pretending to be fine. One day in a rare moment of honesty I admitted to her how wretched I was feeling, that I could not cope with these deaths of my father and step-father in such quick succession. I could not see a way forward, I confessed. She suddenly lost her temper and snapped back at me, 'For God's sake, pull yourself together. My father walked out on me and Mum when I was four. You're not the only person in the world not to have a father. Stop making such a big deal of it.' I was astounded. How could she be so cruel? So incredibly unsympathetic?

Later on I was able to see that maybe she was right, maybe she had been bereaved in a way when her parents separated. To a four-year-old that probably felt like a dreadful loss. Perhaps the sense of being unentitled to your feelings is just as great when you lose a parent that way and at that age; certainly other people are less sympathetic than when there is something clear and unambiguous like a death. With time I could see how my friend's feelings of loss must have been reactivated by my situation and I could understand her angry, impatient outburst, but our friendship never recovered from her inability to tolerate my sorrow.

Usually, however, lack of sympathy and support from friends is due simply to ignorance. The problem of how to cope with bereavement at an age when so few of your contemporaries know what you are going through is a very real one. You are out of sync with your peers and not much can be done to change that. Your needs are very different from those of your friends. You can find yourself very much at odds with people of your own age, with people who in other circumstances were, are or would be your friends. You are highly sensitized to a whole dimension of life that to them is still theoretical, abstract, impersonal, an easy source of humour, not the painful reality that leaves you often in or close to tears.

I once disgraced myself – I felt – when I went to the cinema with a group of friends whom I hadn't known for long and didn't know very well. The film was very funny, until one of the characters, a man in his mid-forties, had a heart attack and died. While everyone else roared with laughter, I burst into tears. My father had had a heart attack in his late forties; watching the man on the screen was just too near the bone. But I found my outburst very embarrassing and it certainly put a damper on the evening. Others have had similar experiences: a few weeks after Jocelyn's mother died a friend tried cheering her up by taking her to 'Indiana Jones and the Temple of Doom'. She too burst into tears – all the intended 'funny' scenes which involved any violence, threat to life or actual death were just too distressing for her to cope with. 'Once Upon a Time in the West' was so un-funny to another bereaved girl that she had to leave after the first ten minutes, much to her well-intentioned friend's dismay.

Feeling out of sync with your peer group puts a strain on relationships too. One common effect of a bereavement is to make you fearful of other people dying. Anxiety about a partner, being frightened by separations and absences are very understandable in the circumstances, but can nevertheless cause real problems when it comes to girlfriends and boyfriends. Partners often don't understand; they interpret it as clinginess, over-dependence and over-involvement, and may be scared off by the way they see this fearful reaction. They want to be having fun, not coping with your grief and anxiety. But fun is not particularly easy to have when your world is thrown upside down and turned inside out, when everything around feels dangerous, fragile and unreliable. What do you do? Do you pretend? Do you avoid any connection with other people, so that your needs and fears remain hidden?

There are no easy answers. The only solutions are short-term: be kind to yourself, put your needs high up the scale of priorities, try not to deny your feelings in the hope of pleasing other people. Give yourself time to grieve: it won't go on forever and it is necessary to feel these things now, not store them up for later. As far as navigating your way through the minefield of a relationship – a minefield for all people whatever their age or stage of life, bereaved or not – you can only really aim to be honest with yourself, to accept the way you are feeling, not to compromise too much, not to force yourself to pretend too often. Allow yourself to feel how you feel, and to be the way you need to be. This may not make you great company at times, but friends and partners worth having will understand and make allowances. At least this course of action will allow you to get on with grieving and coming to terms with grief, a process which hiding your feelings gets in the way of, ultimately with the greatest damage to yourself.

Do expect your moods to be unpredictable. You may well find that you cannot tolerate things like dangerous car rides, which your friends are loving. More sinister is the lure of heightened feelings from alcohol, drugs or danger to cut through the flatness of depression. Be careful of these 'tonics' because anything that artificially induces a 'high' will sooner or later be followed by a 'low' and you can easily find yourself on a spiral heading rapidly downwards. This happened to me after my step-father's death. I had had two years of feeling pretty wretched after my father died, and I simply did not have the energy to cope with a second death. The next time someone passed me a joint I took it and found the dreamy blur that filled my head a great relief. But in the long-run marijuana lowers the blood-sugar level and this had two effects: it aggravated my general feelings of unhappiness and lethargy, and it also made me crave sweet starchy foods which boost the sugar levels in the blood. I was a sitting duck for the next person to offer me some amphetamines. The ensuing see-sawing between artificially boosting myself up and artificially slowing myself down quickly became a horrible trap in which I was caught, more drained and more depressed than ever before. On top of a major shock which was already playing havoc with my system, I was in a bad way.

Alcohol, too, can hold a similar escapist appeal. I know plenty of people for whom it became a dangerous friend in the months after a bereavement, when the world at large seemed to have forgotten them and drink was the only ready comfort. But alcohol too is a depressant and addictive, and a hangover is a wretched thing to struggle with on top of the strain of grief.

I'm not here to say don't do this and don't do that, but I would say be cautious. It is particularly difficult when drugs and alcohol seem the way everyone else is having fun, and when they all seem to be managing it so effortlessly. But you are not like everyone else at the moment. Whether or not you feel it, you are in a weakened and fragile state. If something as mild as a comic film can reduce you to tears, think what something as potent as drink can do. These things may make others laugh, but they are considerably more robust than you right now. If you were driving a Reliant Robin and your friends were in four-wheel drive Land Rovers, would you go on a rally just because they were?

• Coping with family conflict

Strife between you and your family may also be considerable

in this period. All of you are dealing with your own private feelings and inevitably your needs will be different. There is always room for tension in any family and at a time of such stress as this it is not surprising.

There may, for example, be conflict – expressed or concealed – about the role of older siblings, relatives or family friends who have stepped in as kind of surrogate parent. You may resent this intrusion into your privacy and domestic routine. The 'helpful' words and deeds of an aunt, uncle or friend of the family may seem to you interfering, intrusive and wholly unwelcome. The unwanted presence may increase your feelings that your life has been disrupted and destroyed by death and that nothing will ever be good again. For you, it may make matters worse not better that a neighbour cooks supper for you all, or that an uncle now helps your mother with bills and accounts. For you, your parent is irreplaceable and these pseudo-parents only emphasize what you have lost. In no way do they begin to make up for it. Your resentment, anger, irritability and hostility are not easy feelings to cope with, but neither are they entirely unreasonable in the circumstances: it is understandable that a person stepping into your dead parent's shoes should be more an irritating presence than a soothing one to you. They stand, literally, for what you have lost. They represent all that you have lost and can no longer have. It is natural not to welcome them with open arms, even if you can accept that they are helping in practical ways. The fact that they are there at all reminds you that others are not.

It is important in this situation to try to hold both realities in mind: the fact that you do not want a surrogate parent, and the fact that you and your family may really need the practical help that this person can give, be they brother, sister, uncle, aunt or neighbour. Allow yourself to appreciate their help and good intentions, but equally you can allow yourself your feelings of hostility and resentment: they are a valid part of your grief, an expression of the anger that you feel. After all your world has been overturned and undergone these profoundly unwanted changes. You need not act on these feelings, but neither do you need to deny their existence.

The main thing is not to feel guilty for feeling as you do – even if it sets you apart from other relatives. Work out as calmly and clearly as possible what you need and try to give yourself that without interfering with other people's ways of grieving. It is a time to live and let live. Try not to blame yourself for what you are feeling, but try not to get too entangled with other people's feelings either.

More difficult to handle are the after-effects of a complicated relationship with the parent who has died. Tony Walter, in his book *Funerals – and How to Improve Them*, makes the point that: 'It is not the quality but the intensity of the relationship with the deceased that is crucial, and the hardest grief can be for those close family members with whom you did not get on.'

Jane always argued with her mother, and when her mother died Jane was left with dreadful feelings of guilt, imagining that she had made life so difficult at home for everyone, and that she might somehow have caused her mother's cancer by being so quarrelsome. The phrase 'you'll be the death of me' suddenly sounded quite different to Jane's ears.

Sean, on the other hand, had a very cool relationship with his mother and was very close to his father. When his father died he was left feeling guilty that he had not been nicer to his

107

mother who was now all he had. He also felt guilty for secretly wishing his mother had died and not his father.

Another cause for strife at this time can come when there are step-parents or step-children in the family. A step-parent may well have brought you up from an early age and been a crucial figure in your life, but you may find after his or her death that your grief is somehow invalidated because you were not blood relatives. I know how hurt I was when in the obituary for my step-father I read that he would be mourned by 'his widow and four children'. What about me and my brother? Did we not count? Had we not loved him too? Had we not been loved by him? Had he not taken us to and fetched us from school, bathed us, fed us, read us bedtime stories, picked us up when we fell, cuddled us when we cried? Was he not a father to us too? Were we not entitled then to mourn the man who had brought us up for the last fifteen years? Was our grief to be dismissed so easily?

Nor were careless journalists the only ones to dismiss my sorrow and loss: friends and relatives also somehow seemed to assume that I felt less because he was 'only' my step-father. Yet as Tony Walter points out, often we grieve hardest for those whom we may have had difficulties loving, and between step-parents and step-children the bonds of affection are often extremely complicated – a maze of dependence, gratitude, love, anger, resentment, hostility: a whole hotch-potch of negative and positive emotions that can make the grief you feel when they die all the more difficult to cope with.

The fact that society can often fail to recognize the very powerful – though not straightforward – bonds between step-relatives can be an additional source of pain and anger at an already difficult time. Step-siblings can be regarded as more affected by the step-parent's death than you; you may feel your relationship with your step-parent is overlooked. This is incredibly painful and distressing, when it happens, and the first thing you must do in this situation is to tell yourself that whatever anyone else thinks, you are entitled to your grief too.

There is also the possibility that your blood-parent may have been the one to die, leaving you with a step-parent for whom you may have ambivalent feelings or with whom you have a strained relationship. In this case, you may well have to cope with emotions and thoughts that seem unacceptable and shameful: Why didn't your step-parent die instead? Maybe he/she was responsible for the death in some way – maybe if the ambulance had been called sooner, or your parent had been made to lose weight, to stop smoking . . . All kinds of feelings of suspicion and hostility towards a step-parent that have been hidden away for years and years can come flooding back to the surface in the aftermath of a parent's death. And if you are still dependent on your step-parent for a home, food, financial support and so on, the sensation of being both abandoned and trapped can be very distressing. After all, maybe you never even wanted this person in your life, and now you're somehow stuck with them for good. Even if you are financially independent, you may feel responsible for a step-parent after a parent's death. Wanted or not, the emotional ties to a step-parent can be strong. They now represent your links with the parent who has died; you may feel that you need them now in some way. If you break away from them, you will risk losing still more of your links with your dead parent.

Whatever the relationship with your step-parent, there are

bound to be some conflicting and ambivalent feelings to cope with. There are specialized organizations to help you understand the complex emotional ties within step-families (see pp. 265-268) and it may be worth your while contacting them for support. For the time being, it is important that you recognize and accept the validity and reality of what you are feeling – no one has the right to deny you that, or to tell you what you should or should not feel. Give yourself permission to be angry, frightened, lonely, resentful. Give yourself permission to mourn the loss of a step-parent who mattered to you, and give yourself permission to have mixed feelings about a step-parent you are now left with. A bereavement may provide an opportunity to look honestly at emotions that have never before seen the light of day. The best thing you can do at this stage is be honest with yourself; accept your reaction to your parent's death, and give some room to all the conflicting, contradictory, negative emotions and thoughts that may well be troubling you. They have their place in your life, just as the person you have lost had.

Tensions and conflicts are hard to accept, but they are part of the normal process of developing from a childish to a more adult relationship with your parents. What is not normal is their death, which has left you stranded in the middle of this process, with a tangle of thoughts and feelings to deal with. The only way to sort out a complicated relationship with a parent is time. It can seem appallingly unfair that while your friends have this time, and can carry on developing and untangling their relationship with their parents or step-parents well into their twenties and thirties, you have been left with a hell of a mess on your hands and no more time in which to sort it out. In fact, there *are* ways of resolving difficulties

110

with dead parents, as well as living ones, and there *are* ways of finding the time which you feel has been irretrievably lost. These are dealt with later in Chapter 10: Letting go and getting on.

5 Mourning time: the second year and after

> 'It is impossible to think that I
> shall never sit with you again
> and hear your laugh. That every
> day for the rest of my life you
> will be away.'
> (Dora Carrington)

After about a year life should begin to settle down again, and the new routines begin to feel a bit more familiar. It is also, however, a time when support will probably have stopped, and you will have to find ways of dealing alone with the inevitable resurgence of pain and grief.

• Anniversaries

The beginning of the second year is marked by the first anniversary of your parent's death, an occasion which you may well find upsetting. Significant events in the years after a parent's death can be surprisingly hard to deal with, particularly these 'firsts': the first Christmas, the first birthday, the first holiday. These events, and none more than the first anniversary, are reminders that life is continuing for you without your parent and a reminder of what you have lost and of how you have changed. The newly bereaved are like children starting to learn how to live in a strange and unfamiliar land. These landmarks remind you of what you once knew and of just how strange and unfamiliar the new things still are to you.

Anniversaries are a particularly poignant reminder, not only this first one, but each anniversary for many years will revive feelings and thoughts that for the rest of the year you may be able to forget. Memories of how your parent died, the place where it happened, where you were at the time, how you felt when you found out about the death, the events surrounding the death – all these are stirred up again by this annual event.

The first few years after my father and step-father died, I felt very alone with my sadness and loss on the anniversaries of their deaths. Although people who did remember were nice to my mother on that day, few seemed to realize that it was a sad day for me too, that I could also have done with a sympathetic phone call or letter to help me through the day.

The first anniversary of my father's death fell, appropriately, on the day of his memorial service, so I did have communal support. In addition, Tim, the boyfriend who had been with me the day twelve months before when I heard the news, did remember and sent me a letter, which I greatly appreciated, both in itself and for the thoughtfulness behind it. But as time goes on, the chances of this kind of recognition decrease and it can be left entirely to you to decide whether to mark or ignore the anniversary. Sometimes you may feel considerable pressure from others not to mark the death of your parent but to hurry up and forget about it.

I remember one evening a few years after my father's

114

death being invited out to dinner. I arrived early and was sitting in the kitchen with my host while he finished off the cooking.

'So how are things with you?' he asked.

'Well, OK.' I replied. 'A little sad today because it's the anniversary of my father's death.' There was a short silence, then Greg said, 'But that was years ago. You can't keep on feeling sad about it.' It was my turn to be surprised – and annoyed. 'I don't want to feel this way,' I said. 'I just do. I can't help it.'

It isn't always easy but my policy over the years has been not to worry too much about other people's attitudes towards anniversaries. If I want to mention my father, or talk about my feelings for him I do. Sometimes this makes me feel like the proverbial bull in a china shop, but I try to protect my right to speak when I want or need to. I usually try to tell people it is the anniversary, and let them take care of their own reaction. After all, why should I pretend it is a day like any other? For me, it's not.

However much pressure you feel to ignore the anniversary, the likelihood is that you will be aware of it anyway. This isn't so strange when you think about it: you would hardly forget your own birthday, regardless of whether other people remembered it or not, and this day too is a significant one in your life. Along with your birthday it probably affected you more than any other day in your life so far. It is not so easy to forget a parent's death or the anniversary of it as people sometimes suppose.

Janet rang her mother the night before the anniversary of her father's death. She later recounted the conversation to me as follows:

'Hi Mum, I'm just calling because I won't be able to tomorrow, but I will be thinking about you.'

'That's nice of you, but it's a long time ago now and actually I don't get sad any more.'

'Don't you? Oh, well, good.' There was a pause in the conversation, then Janet asked, 'So how have you been?'

'Oh, you know: too much work. I must say, though, I've been feeling quite depressed this week. I can't think why.'

'And how's Henry?' [her mother's new husband]

'Henry's fine. But I had an awful experience this morning. I walked into the living-room where he was sitting reading the paper and for a moment I was convinced it was Peter sitting there instead. It was uncannily real. I can't think why I should suddenly imagine such a thing.'

'Maybe you're more aware that tomorrow's the 15th of April than you think.' There was a little silence at the other end, then her mother laughed. 'Yes, maybe I am!'

Ed's approach to anniversaries is quite different from Janet's mother's. He was twenty-one when his mother died. He says he is always aware when the anniversary is coming round. This year he and his family have decided to go back to the place in the country where his mother died, and mark the anniversary by being together that day and lighting candles in remembrance of her life. Ed says he is looking forward to it: he would rather be sharing sad and happy moments in the supportive company of friends and family, than on his own pretending it is a day like any other.

Formal recognition of an anniversary can be very helpful, whether it is an event organized for close family, or a public memorial service. Religious communities can play an important part here too. I have already described the Jewish custom of observing the *Jahrzeit* where the name of the dead person is read out in synagogue and a special prayer said each year around the time of their death (see p.79). Other religions, though the custom is less institutionalized, will also

116

do this at their meetings and services and if it helps you, then do ask your priest to mention your parent by name at the service nearest to their anniversary.

But marked formally or not, anniversaries do not usually go privately unmarked. I find myself very aware of the anniversary whether or not I want to be, and with time I have decided it is not worth fighting this awareness. It is probably better to mark the day and use it as an occasion to be conscious of my father or step-father, than to try and pretend it is just a day like any other. Loss and life deserve and need to be marked. Trying to ignore the event only makes it harder to bear. Anniversaries are an opportunity to remember, not a curse; they should be used not denied.

The second year is when major changes often take place, which can unexpectedly reawaken painful feelings you had thought were over at last. Moving house, remarriage, changing jobs, are all things which may well happen in the second year of bereavement. In the first year people usually avoid any major changes. Instinctively you want to be still and not rock the already unsteady boat. But after a year this is no longer practical or necessary. Perhaps financial pressures force a house move. Perhaps the remaining parent decides to marry again. It is important to realize that all change involves loss and that all change will have the power to reactivate old feelings of loss, (this is described in detail in Chapters 6 and 7). The best way to help yourself through these changes is to be very honest in recognizing what you are losing, and to allow yourself to be sad for that loss.

Johnny's mother died when he was twenty-two. A year later his father remarried and moved house. Since Johnny no

117

longer lived at home, he felt unentitled to his feelings of sadness and loss, and unable to express his ambivalence about these changes. Determined to be positive about these changes and see the good side, Johnny could not allow himself to feel sad for the loss of the old home where he had lived all his life and which was intimately bound up with the memory of his mother. Nor did he accept how torn he felt about his father's remarriage. Instead he suppressed feelings of sadness, anger and fear, which came out later in self-destructive ways when he began drinking too much. He kept winding up in hopeless relationships, and found himself prone to bouts of deep despondency that left him despairing of ever getting over his mother's death.

It is vitally important to recognize that for you the repercussions of these changes in the second year may be quite serious. Allow yourself to see what you are losing and try if possible to take your feelings seriously. Pretending to yourself and other people to be coping fine now will not help you in the long run if your feelings are really much more complicated than that. It is vital not to impose a strict and arbitrary cut-off line on your grief, after which you do not let yourself mourn, because the effects of a parent's death will continue to make themselves felt for at least two years, and possibly longer. You must allow yourself this mourning time, for as long as you need it.

• Physical symptoms of grief

The basic 'timetable' for mourning gives you some idea of the kinds of emotions that are likely to occur at different stages in the two years after a parent's death, but grief often emerges as a physical reaction too. Emotions do not exist in a vacuum, they take place in the container of the body and very often emotional and physical reactions to a death are indistinguishable from one another. On top of the more obvious feelings you will have after a death, such as anger, guilt, sadness, irritability, fear and anxiety, you will also experience many other emotions as physical symptoms. You may well feel and be weepy, easily reduced to tears or unexpectedly bursting into tears. You may be lethargic, unable to drag yourself through the day and lacking in energy, or else you may be restless, unable to concentrate or settle to anything. A sensation of hollowness can be both a physical sensation in your stomach and an emotional emptiness.

You may have physical symptoms which do not obviously relate to an emotion. Not being able to sleep, having recurrent bad dreams and nightmares, sweating or shaky hands and nervous tics are all physical displays of hidden emotions. Anxiety can cause headaches, sweating, trembling or nausea. It is not uncommon to feel literally heavy-hearted when you are mourning the loss of a parent, or for the area around your heart to ache. Sadness can often feel like sickness.

When Martin's mother died of stomach cancer he was nineteen. He was gripped with a feeling of sickness in his own stomach which lasted almost continuously for a year after her death. Tom, on the other hand, learnt to recognize in his trembling hands his concern that he would not be able to hold things together now that his father was dead and so much responsibility fell into his hands.

Shock is like an illness itself – physical and emotional. People in shock need to stay still, keep warm and rest. After an accident people are often reported to be suffering from shock. It wasn't until I was mugged one night walking home from the bus stop that I realized that 'suffering from shock' is not a vague phrase, like 'under the weather', it describes a specific set of reactions: feeling very cold and shivery, confusion, sleeplessness, panic attacks, inability to settle down or concentrate on anything, even the TV or paper. I also erupted in spots and had aches and pains all over my body. Emotional shock too can bring on all these reactions and it needs the same care and attention. Unfortunately people are not very good at recognizing this either in themselves or others. Instead they try to keep busy, distract themselves. Often it takes a more obvious physical illness or an accident to make people rest, stay still, realizing that they are frail and vulnerable after someone has died. Lily Pincus, in her book *Death in the Family*, describes how she fractured her ankle after her husband's death. While she was being treated she asked the orthopaedic surgeon if it was common for people to fracture bones after bereavement. The doctor replied 'without even looking up from my foot, "Naturally, people lose their sense of balance".'

Recurrences of old illnesses are also not uncommon when you are in this vulnerable state, nor is increased susceptibility to colds, coughs and bouts of flu. You are weakened physically as well as emotionally by shock. It is not morbid or unhealthy or self-indulgent to care for yourself, swaddle yourself, convalesce after a major shock like bereavement. It is necessary and sensible.

Sometimes your body can tell you more about how you are feeling than your mind can. Physical symptoms are very much part of how you mourn for someone you love. It is common, though distressing, to imagine you have the symptoms that your dead parent had – tightness in the chest or pains in the head. This is part of how you continue to feel connected to someone when he or she has died: physically you empathize with their situation so much that you can sometimes start to feel as you imagine they felt. These sensations almost always pass with time.

Sometimes you may experience physical symptoms and emotions that are not always easy to understand. When the cause is particularly complicated or deeply suppressed, for whatever reasons, you may find that you are projecting feelings out into the world, rather than feeling them inside you. It is as if you have turned the world, or sometimes just one aspect of it, into a great white screen, on to which you then throw – often without realizing it – the image of your most hidden feelings and fears.

David was twenty-one when his father died. They had had a close but complicated relationship. Even while his father was alive, David often felt that his father was over-ambitious for him, unduly critical and impossible to please. After his father's death, he became obsessed with cleanliness, washing his hands over and over again in the course of the day. He also became obsessed with the hidden danger of asbestos, convinced that the rooms he was in were full of poisonous asbestos fumes which were seeping into him. On one occasion he became so panic-stricken about this invisible threat that he rang his sister and pleaded with her to come to his flat to check it over for asbestos.

What David was projecting on to the world was his own secret fear that something in him was bad and destructive. Secretly he feared that this hidden 'poison' that he sensed all around him was already inside him. The more he worried that

121

he was in fact the source of this poison, the more frantically he tried to find it in some source outside himself. The 'poison' he so feared was several things: unexpressed anger that he had often felt towards his father for being so critical of him; the irrational fantasy that this anger had somehow killed his father; and the fear that his father had been right to be so critical and that he, David, was a bad person not deserving of approval or praise, in fact capable of terrible destruction.

Fiona had a milder form of the same type of deeply hidden feelings and fears. After her mother's death she became very sensitive to 'bad' smells, imagining she could detect dog shit or sewage everywhere she went. After a few months the acute awareness of unpleasant smells faded back to normal, but Fiona began to realize that this heightened sensitivity to smell recurred whenever she was feeling anxious or worried or under pressure. With the help of a therapist, whom she was seeing to help with her feelings after her mother's death, Fiona eventually remembered that she had suffered from the same obsession with smells as a child around the time when her parents had divorced and her father left home. For Fiona, imagining that she could smell something rotten and bad was a way of expressing her own fears that she herself was the bad, rotten presence which first her father and later her mother had not wanted to be near. It was her own fear that she was not good, not nice to be near, that she could smell.

For both David and Fiona these complicated reactions were triggered, though not exactly caused, by grief and took a long time to untangle. Though not always in such extreme forms, everyone will have these childhood fears which in adulthood require sorting out, looking at and dealing with. Often this process involves learning to see your parents and yourself more objectively, more kindly, in order to understand why they behaved as they did and why you reacted as you did. The trouble for those who are still young when parents die is that it makes this process much more difficult. It is easy to get stuck at a certain point in relation to your parents – both the living and the dead – and that point is often still caught up in childhood. You were just beginning to disentangle yourself from that and start to build an adult relationship with them and with yourself, when suddenly the goalposts were shifted – or rather the referee blew the whistle and ended the game. What you have to do – and it is not at all an easy task – is to find ways of playing the game still in your imagination, so that even though your parent is no longer alive to help, you can still let go of the child inside you and continue to develop that adult relationship with yourself and your parent, which you were about to build or were in the process of building. On top of mourning a parent's death this is quite a daunting business, and it does take time.

• Complications

Sometimes the two-year process of mourning is complicated by other factors, perhaps your personal circumstances or perhaps events beyond your control.

In *Grief Counselling and Grief Therapy*, J. William Worden outlines the factors which may delay or complicate mourning as follows:

1 Your relationship with the person who has died: how difficult was your relationship; how ambivalent did you feel about the

person; how involved with the person were you and how dependent on the relationship?

2 The circumstances of the death: is the death certain or only supposed; is the death part of a larger event in which many other people also died?

3 Your personal history: do you have other experiences of traumatic or repeated loss or separation in the past?

4 Your personality: are you an optimistic or pessimistic type of person; do you regard yourself as a strong or weak person, an activator or a victim of events; do you find fluctuations in mood bearable or do you prefer to be in control of your emotions?

5 Society's response: are you able to talk freely about your feelings and about the person who has died with friends and family; is the death seen as shameful by society, as often happens in the case of suicide; is the death simply not recognized as a death by society, as in the case of abortions and miscarriages; is the death not known about by other people and are you therefore without any forms of support?

It is worth asking yourself some of these questions so that you have some idea of what your needs are likely to be. This in turn will help you to understand all the ramifications and likely repercussions of this bereavement in your life in the time ahead.

As well as the factors that Worden lists, there is also the effect of another loss or death within the first two years after a parent's death. Two years might have been long enough for me if my step-father had not also died within that time. Lady Bracknell's famous comment in *The Importance of Being Earnest* about it being unfortunate to lose one parent, but carelessness to lose two suddenly sounded less amusing to my ears!

Unfortunately, it is not uncommon for other significant losses to take place within a short space of time. In some cases this is another death. Research has shown that widows and widowers have a higher risk of death within a year of their partner dying than unbereaved people of the same age.

After my father's death I became friendly with a fellow student called Angela whose father had also died of a heart attack. One week a few months later she did not turn up at the time we had planned to meet. I went round to her room a few days later to make sure she was all right. She wasn't. Her mother had committed suicide, she told me, her voice flat, her face bright and empty with shock.

Emma Judge, writing in the *Guardian*, describes how her father died of a heart attack at Easter and her mother died of cancer five months later. Her mother had already been diagnosed as terminally ill before her father's death and as Emma writes, 'Dad had been the main prop for us all while Mum was ill. He looked after her, went to all the doctors with her and comforted her. We all turned to him to know what to do. My family gathered at our house after he died; we just didn't know what to do. It was the worst day of my life.'

Even if there are other relatives around to offer love and kindness and support, the death of both your parents within a short space of time is a terrible, terrible tragedy.

Maybe, however, it is not the death of another parent, but of a friend or relative.

Justin had to cope with the death of his beloved

125

grandmother and then his father within six months of each other. Kate heard that a friend of hers had been killed in a car crash and, coming soon after her father's death, this affected her very deeply even though the friend had not been an especially close one.

For Nicola it was getting pregnant and having to have an abortion that came as another intolerable loss while she was still reeling from her mother's death. In Nicola's case this second loss made it impossible for her to carry on 'coping' on her own and she sought support from a professional counsellor.

In the months following a bereavement, you will be extra-sensitive to death and to loss. It is like losing a layer of skin: you will be red-raw to anything that rubs up against you thereafter. I found I could not even bear to read reports of major disasters in the paper. Watching interviews on television news with people whose relatives had been killed in the fire at the Bradford football stadium reduced me to tears. When a nineteen year old girl was murdered not far from where I live, the papers carried pictures of her family coming out of the funeral. I found their grief-worn faces unbearably moving.

Any new and direct experience of death when you are still so weakened from the first death can set you back. It reactivates the feelings of fear and vulnerability and helplessness that first engulf you when someone you love dies. But you will also be sensitive to other kinds of losses, such as the loss of a job or a family home, or the loss of a parent through remarriage. All sorts of things can knock you off balance again, just as you thought you were getting yourself upright once more. Loss throughout your life will have the power to reactivate feelings connected with earlier losses (*see* Chapter 8: Old grief in new guises), but these are different from major losses that occur within the two-year period of mourning. Future losses will be painful, but it is these ill-timed unavoidable losses that happen at this stage that can radically affect your ability to mourn and to heal, and which must therefore be taken very seriously. It will help if you can see them as losses and not be hard on yourself for being more affected by them than you imagine you 'ought' to be.

• Getting support

You may well find yourself needing more support than you are getting from friends and family during the two years after a parent's death. As the sociologist Geoffrey Gorer wrote after carrying out his classic research into bereavement and mourning in Britain in the sixties: 'Human beings mourn in response to grief, and . . . if mourning is denied outlet, the result will be suffering, either psychological or physical or both.'

Given how little recognition there is of the needs of young people whose parents have died, it is not improbable that your grief will be denied outlet, at some stage and to some degree.

After my father and step-father died, I became very aware of how little support was actually available for people in my position: young people trying to establish their own lives at the same time as trying to come to terms with the death of a parent. My tutors were sympathetic but left it to me to go to them – something I did not feel able to do. I didn't want to talk to the university help-line because it was run by students and I didn't think they would understand what I was going through.

127

Anyway, I thought, that was for people with essay crises and problems with relationships, not for real, serious situations like bereavement. The university did have a counselling service but again, the onus was on me to make an appointment and get myself there. I would think about it when I was feeling really low, but then I'd think: 'Well, leave it a day and I might feel a bit better in the morning.' And the next morning I wouldn't feel much better but I would have persuaded myself I was making a fuss about nothing, that there was nothing anyone could say or do to help anyway – since they couldn't do the one thing I really wanted and bring back the dead. If the counsellors had approached me, I might have gone to see them. As it was, I never did.

The situation has improved in the last ten years and there are now various organizations which provide counselling for bereaved young people, both locally and nationally. Otherwise there are professional therapists and counsellors. (Lists of these organizations and how to contact them are given on p.265-268)

However, the burden is usually still on you to make the first move; if you want support, you have to find it, and after a parent's death this may feel like the last thing you want or are able to do. The idea of making yourself more vulnerable than you already are by going and talking to someone can be really frightening. You may feel you will be stirring up painful feelings that are best left alone. But it is essential that you are straight with yourself: are you really OK? Are you really managing without anyone to talk to or share your feelings with? However frightening the idea of talking about your grief and sorrow and loss may seem, is it really worse than carrying it around in the back of your mind like a great dark shadow the

128

whole time, hoping it will have gone next time you look, but never quite daring to look in case it hasn't?

The idea of talking to a stranger may seem daunting, but it can be an immense relief to share what you are going through with someone qualified to help and experienced in the painful, lonely ways of bereavement. There is nothing to be gained from loneliness. Finding an understanding ear to talk to will make you feel far less isolated, far less different than you may imagine you are. Talking to other people really can help. While you have not been through this experience before, other people have and they will understand that talking helps and will not consider it a sign of weakness, as you may fear it is.

Don't be put off by the stigma of seeing a professional. Once may be enough. If not, then don't be afraid to seek out understanding company or support whenever you need it – once a month, once a week, once a day. It doesn't matter. It is not shameful to need support. In other cultures throughout the world people are allowed to sit and talk and weep for their loved ones. Only our modern Western culture insists on tidying up sorrow and burying it – preferably at the same time as burying the corpse. If you really can't find anyone to talk to, but need some kind of support, try books. There are kind voices to be heard there too. And although not many books deal specifically with the effect of a parent's death when you are in your teens or twenties, some of the other books available do address the general experience of bereavement with great sensitivity. Or you may find other ways, apart from talking, to relieve the burden of troubling thoughts and feelings.

After her mother's death, the main source of comfort for Ruth was her painting. She found she could channel much of her bewilderment and sorrow into art. 'I didn't have anyone to talk to about how I was feeling,' she recalls, 'so it just all came out in my painting. The things appearing on the canvasses were pretty strange, but it was a really important outlet.'

Producing something creative out of such a deadening negative experience helped give Ruth a sense of her own life continuing, of the reality of her existence when everything seemed so unreal. Other people have found the same kind of comfort in playing the piano, writing short stories or a journal, doing pottery or sewing. Doing something, making something out of the dreadful nothingness of a loved parent's absence is a way of filling the void left by their death – the physical, emotional and psychological void.

I used to be amazed and indignant at the assumption that now my father was no longer alive, I should behave as if he never had been. I was expected to stop thinking about him, talking about him, caring about him, needing him, missing him or being influenced or affected by him. People would never have expected me to behave that way if he had simply gone abroad for a few years. It would have seemed perfectly obvious then that his influence over the previous eighteen years would continue to make itself felt. Instead there was a continual tension between my sense of his absence which I neither liked nor wanted, and other people's insistence that I hurry up and forget about him. That is how it felt to me, anyway. Some form of expressive activity in this bewildering time can help to ease the gaping emptiness that you may feel. When it is connected with your emotions at a deep level – as painting or writing or music are – such activities can also help to maintain the links with your parent's influence and presence and importance to you. To have this, when you may feel that you are under tremendous pressure to forget your parent altogether, can be very helpful.

William Worden's suggested two years may sound a long time, but it may not be long enough. It is now more than ten years since my father died and in retrospect I can see that it took all of those two years – in fact nearer to five or six years – really to accept that he was dead, really admit the anguish of losing him, and really begin to live my life with this knowledge. Until then I was petrified of going into the future, regarding myself as a still-wounded and frail victim of bereavement. Instead of struggling against the fact of his death, not wanting or daring to let go of the past because the past was where he was, I found gradually it was possible to take the fact of his death and the continuing memory of him with me more comfortably into the future.

For most young people, the death of a parent and the two years thereafter will usually coincide with big changes taking place. Whereas widows and widowers in their forties or fifties are likely to have a settled way of life behind and before them, someone of seventeen, twenty or twenty-three is probably going to be coping with a whole set of dramatic changes on top of the changes caused by death. The two years of mourning will coincide with leaving home for the first time, going to college, starting a new job, taking exams, maybe even getting married or having a child. These events, however wanted and necessary, nevertheless interfere with the natural process of mourning and sometimes make it very difficult to do the necessary work of getting used to a death. And it is work. Hard work. It takes time and energy and courage and honesty. To have to do this 'work' at the same time as starting your first job, or living away from home for the first time can simply be too much.

Coping with these double demands is dealt with in detail in the next chapter. It is important to recognize the additional pressures that you are having to deal with at the same time as coming to terms with death, and this coincidence of major changes may mean that for you the whole process of mourning will take much longer than two years.

As far as possible try to be patient with yourself – recognize that your needs are important, that they are different from those of your remaining parent, grandparents, aunts and uncles, and also that your needs are different from those of your friends. Be honest about what you are feeling and thinking and do try to have faith in the fact that you *will* find a meaning for this tragic event, that you *will* be able to make a place in your life both for your dead parent and for the fact of his or her death. Try to remember that it does take time and the only person able to give you permission to take that time is you.

In the first two years there will be moments when it may seem extraordinarily hard to believe that you are getting used to the death of your parent, that depression and feelings of hopelessness are really a sign that you are fairly far down the road to recovery (whatever 'recovery' means to you). All you can do is trust in the experience of other people that this is so, that this despair you feel is the final frost before the spring.

These weeks, months and years without the parent you love and need can seem unbearable, but usually with time you find that somehow you have borne them. Be kind and gentle with yourself in the meantime and try not to look too far ahead; just take one step at a time. The night is always darkest, it is said, in the hour before the dawn.

6 Changes and losses – the private kind

'Every entrance is also an exit.
Every gain is also a loss.'
(Audrey T. McCollum)

These years in your teens and early twenties are full of changes and losses, quite apart from the change and loss that comes with a parent's death. Losing a job is a kind of bereavement, so is losing a group of schoolfriends, or losing your family home. Breaking up with a partner is a loss that can feel like a bereavement. Losing possessions can be upsetting too – a favourite book, a special piece of jewellery, a prized record, these things can be important and the loss of them can be distressing.

In her book, *Counselling Young People*, E. Doolan describes this stage in life as a period of transition similar in many respects to bereavement; one which involves losing aspects of yourself and mourning for that loss. Mood swings, anger, guilt, depression, impatience and impetuousness are all emotional states common, she says, to the bereaved and to the adolescent. Her analogy highlights one of the major difficulties for people whose parents die when they are still young: you are *already* going through a kind of bereavement, losing parts of yourself and the people around you. A parent's death at the same time is a double blow, an additional loss and shock in a time of already considerable shock and loss.

Getting used to a parent's death involves changes and loss in the way we view ourselves and the world; so does making the transition from childhood to adulthood. It is a transition from one stage of life with one set of issues to a stage of life with another set, not in itself worse or better, but all the same different. Anything different involves change, and any kind of change, however welcome, however wanted, however longed-for, involves loss. It is important not to overestimate your ability to cope with change after a parent's death, not to overlook the fact that these changes incur losses which in turn may reactivate old grief.

Imagine, for instance, going into a bookshop and selecting a book: you go to the counter, hand over the money, walk out with the book. You have what you wanted: you have changed money for a book, but you have also lost something: the money. There's no way to avoid it. Change always involves loss. Even to choose between two pairs of shoes involves losing the pair you decide not to buy. From the most banal to the most significant examples, change entails loss. And loss for those who have had a parent die recently can be very painful and upsetting.

You may want to leave home, you may want to go to college, you may want to get married, you may want to move into your own flat. All these things you may genuinely want and need to do, but they will involve loss as well as gain. If you can spare enough time to anticipate what you will be losing, it will come as less of a shock, and be easier to deal with. To feel sad, lonely, depressed or angry as a result of a change in your life is not peculiar, it is not a sign of failure, it is called adjusting.

Modern society allows ever less time for things: trains and cars are getting faster, book-jackets must grab our attention in a matter of seconds, we spend increasingly less time cooking and cleaning because gadgets and inventions do these things for us. As a result of all this time-saving and speeding-up, we are free to get on with doing more things more quickly with the rest of our time! But adjusting to major change won't be hurried along by modern technology: it takes as much time as it needs. Adjusting is a process of settling into a new niche, seeing how it fits, where it rubs, where it is snug, how it feels. It is like wearing in a new pair of shoes. Take a significant event in your life, like moving house, leaving your family, starting your first job, and the period of adjustment will be correspondingly more complicated, lengthy and subtle.

When a parent dies it leaves a gap not only inside you, but also in the world you live in. This is horribly obvious: each time you see the empty chair at the table, the unused umbrella in the hall, you face the gap in your life now. I remember bringing my mother a cup of tea in bed one morning after my step-father died and being quite shocked at how small she looked in the big half-empty bed. How much bigger it must have felt to her without my large, bear-like step-father lying there beside her.

A parent's death will nearly always be the catalyst for a whole series of changes in your life, internally and externally. It can often seem as if nothing is left untouched by death. But on top of the vast change caused by your parent's death alone, all these extra changes can sometimes feel unbearable. The gaps left in your daily life after a parent's death are hard to tolerate at first. You miss the voice in the hall, the face at the door, the kiss at bedtime. And then gradually you and your family begin to shift about a bit, rearrange yourselves to fill those gaps. Somebody else makes supper or washes it up; somebody else takes charge of emptying the bins or putting out the milk bottles. Somebody else now takes the car to be serviced or weeds the garden. Somebody else buys the newspaper on Sunday mornings.

Sometimes these changes make life easier: it can be reassuring for life to start functioning again, for the chaos after a death to be coming to an end. These daily routines and rituals can keep you going, renew your confidence in the world and in life, distract you from the sadness you are feeling. But sometimes these changes can be distressing, making you feel that the person you love has been easily dismissed, replaced, their death forgotten.

Sometimes the changes do not make things 'as before', but instead underline how very different life is now.

In our house life changed dramatically after my step-father's death. My mother had a full-time job; household work previously done by my step-father was simply left undone. I had left home by then and noticed when I visited how much messier everything was. Mealtimes were no longer friendly, civilized events, they were now rushed, haphazard affairs, everyone eating in silence and hurrying back to whatever they'd been doing before. No one seemed to be communicating. We all just lived in our own little bubbles alongside one another. In general, there was far less order in the house as it was hard for my mother to maintain much discipline without her husband to help; regular bedtimes went out of the window along with any kind of rules about friends coming round. It was all very chaotic and I did not like it a bit. Far from feeling sympathy for my mother for having so much to worry about, I felt angry with her for not protecting us from so much unwanted change. I wanted things as they had been.

It is *essential* to make changes in your life, to take risks, to try new things, but it is equally important – and I talk as the fool who invariably rushed in – to look at the *loss* involved in change as well as the gain. It is important to expect and allow time to mourn for what is being lost as a result of these changes, and expect and allow past feelings of loss to re-emerge. To lose things that matter to you is to lose a little part of yourself; when you have already lost rather a large part of yourself through your parent's death, even quite small later losses can reopen the old wounds. On top of the pain of the new loss you feel all over again the pain of the old one. You need to work out what it is you are losing and mourn for it.

There are basically two kinds of change and it can be helpful to differentiate between the two.

The first are the changes that come as a direct result of your parent's death and in its immediate wake. These changes involve losses which may be vividly evident to you but may not be so obvious to anyone else, such as a loss of routine, a loss of confidence, a sense of having lost your youth, and, perhaps most painful of all, the feeling that you have lost your living parent too.

The second kind of changes are those that come as a matter of course, but which are particularly hard for you to handle because of your parent's death, such as moving house, changing job, or ending a relationship. These changes are clearly visible to everyone, but what is not always evident to other people is that you may experience these changes primarily as painful losses.

This chapter and the one following look at each of these kinds of change in turn, and at the losses they may involve.

• Changing roles

One of the most difficult changes that takes place after a parent dies is the change in roles within the family. These changes are often extremely uncomfortable. You may find yourself mothering your mother or being the 'wife' to your father. Being the brave one or the weak one or the one who 'is coping marvellously' can be a strait-jacket at a time when you need space not restrictions. It is not very helpful to be cast in these roles and often they can make it impossible for you to know or act on what you really think and feel.

Role changes are particularly pronounced and particularly difficult to cope with at this stage in your life. You are already trying to negotiate changes from one role to another whether a parent dies or not, and it is a slow, complicated process. It takes time to find ways to be the grown-up son who can take care of himself, not the little boy whose shoelaces were always undone. It takes time to discover how to be the grown-up daughter who knows perfectly well not to take lifts from strangers. It takes time to learn how to be an adult 'child' in relation to your parents, to see them as people not just parents. This same process is happening with siblings: trying to end fifteen years of unbroken warfare with brothers and sisters is not easy, neither is making the change from bossy older sibling to friend. Outside your family you are also taking on new roles; no longer just a child, you may now also be a wage-earner, home-owner, car-driver, credit card-holder, lover, maybe even a parent yourself.

It can take years and years to negotiate these changes in the way you see yourself and the way you are seen by family and friends. But when a parent dies, there is no time any more. Suddenly you must be able to act as an adult. There is no room anymore for the part of you that still wants to be fifteen or eight, or even four. You lose a part of yourself and you lose it suddenly.

Often you will not only find you have to take responsibility for yourself as never before, but you may well also be taking responsibility for other people too, such as brothers, sisters, the remaining parent, or even friends. Their needs will not always tally with yours.

When her mother died, Paula became a kind of parent to her younger siblings. She had to take them to school, make their tea, talk to them about problems with their teachers, help them with their homework. And she disliked this role intensely. 'I was their sister, I didn't *want* to be a parent to them', she recalls. In the long term it proved impossible to be a sister and a parent-figure. 'Years of quizzing them, in my capacity of pseudo-parent, about schoolwork, life-plans, smoking and drinking, sex and contraception, made a gulf between us. In some ways I lost them as siblings when our mum died.'

But this kind of role reversal is not at all uncommon after the death of a parent. Some or part of the role previously occupied by the dead person in the family will often fall to the oldest son or daughter. Sometimes this role falls to a younger sibling if, for example, she is the only girl in the family and the mother has died, or the only boy after the father has died. Whatever your rank in the family this 'shoe-filling' can create real difficulties: it is deeply confusing to have to 'become' your mother or father at exactly the time when you are trying to work out who you are in your own right.

Saul was only ten when his father died, but the effects of the role he had to play after his father's death lasted throughout his teens and twenties. The youngest of six children and the only son in an Orthodox Jewish family, Saul found himself, at the age of ten, both the man of the household and the baby. His mother's expectations of him were high. He had to be not only her little boy, but husband to her, and father to his older sisters. Furthermore the family's income was dramatically reduced after his father's death and they were forced to move to a smaller house. As the youngest child and only boy, Saul had to sleep in the living-room until he was thirteen. His father's death had at one stroke deprived him of childhood, stability and privacy. From then on Saul was literally and symbolically in the public eye, the focus of everyone's attention. Even his bedroom was a public causeway. At fifteen he left home. At nineteen he left the country. These dramatic breaks were the only way he felt able to escape the pressure of the roles his father's death had left him to fill. He had to cut himself off from his home and country altogether, reject them and make it impossible for his family to reach him, in order to live his own life. He had to have an ocean and a continent between him and them before he felt far enough away to live his life for himself, being who he wanted to be, not acting out a series of roles.

Polly's mother died when she was fifteen; she had two

younger brothers and very much took over running the household. Despite the fact that she was still very young herself, Polly became mother and wife to her brothers and father. At seventeen she abandoned her A levels and at eighteen she got married. Within three years she had two children of her own. Ten years later she 'flipped', as she puts it: she left her husband, went to live abroad and for a while became seriously anorexic: she simply rejected the responsible adult role she had been forced into so early. Being a mother was something she had done without thinking, but as her own children got older and less dependent on her she began to see how little mothering she had had herself, how she wanted and needed to be young and free. She had to break out of her own marriage and family in order to begin to put together an adult life at her own pace.

Sarah, on the other hand, took on her father's role of being the responsible one in the family after his death. She became the caring one, sensitive to everybody else's needs. If this role helped the rest of her family, it certainly wasn't good for her: she put on a lot of weight, became very serious and anxious and unconsciously even began to adopt her dead father's posture and walk. At seventeen she looked bowed down with the weight on her shoulders. Her family didn't object: it was nice for them to feel there was still somebody around with their best interests at heart; it made them feel somehow that their father/husband was still around. 'She's so like her father,' everyone said, as if this were a natural and good way to be. It wasn't until Sarah left home that she realized what had happened and that it was not her responsibility to look after the entire family. She realized that her relationship with her father had centred on his care for her, and that was what she missed.

141

Being him didn't help her to come to terms with missing him, nor to incorporate his importance to her and her love for him into her own life in a way that did not actually prevent her living it.

to It is these shifts in roles within the family that probably begin make you aware of what specifically has been lost since your mother or father died. I have used the general term 'parent', but the death of a mother will affect a family differently from the death of a father, and the feelings of a daughter losing a mother are not the same as a son losing a mother, any more than a daughter's reaction to a father's death is the same as a son's. The organization CRUSE publishes two small leaflets entitled *My Mother Died* and *My Father Died* in recognition of the different roles a parent plays, and in her book, *Coping With Grief,* Susan Wallbank takes some time to go into the varying impact of a parent's death on a son or daughter.

It is important to recognize exactly what you have lost. And although stereotypes are changing within families, mothers and fathers still tend to take traditional roles within the home, which means that when one of them dies, his or her role will be very obviously vacant – and not that easy for the remaining parent to fill. If you are a boy whose mother has died, then you may well feel that the caring, warm, supportive, nurturing, accepting element of your life has gone. For a girl, a mother's death may mean not only those things have gone, but also an ally, a companion, a friend and adviser. When a mother dies, often what goes with her is the secure organized base of your world: there is no one now to ensure the sheets are washed, the cupboards stocked, the bread fresh, your games-kit ready, your school shirts ironed.

When a father dies, a son may feel he has lost an important role model, adviser, guider, encourager, not to mention the person he plays football or cricket with, watches TV with, argues with. There may well also be the loss of the main wage-earner in the family whose death brings financial insecurity too. As the son, you may feel now that it is your responsibilty to provide this leadership and financial security. A daughter, on the other hand, will be losing other things when a father dies: maybe a protector, an admirer, a supporter, a strong male presence to reassure and comfort her in a world where men all too often can seem threatening or frightening.

Ironically, even if your parent was not these things in life, you may still miss them after he or she has died. A mother who was neglectful, critical and unsupportive while she was alive may by dying, rouse great longings in you for the very opposite charactcristics from thosc shc actually cmbodicd. Similarly the death of an aggressive or a distant father can make you crave still more the father of your dreams who would nurture and protect you. It is as if by dying your mother or father has taken away forever the possibility of ever having those things. However strange it sounds, you can miss both the things your parent was and the things he or she failed to be.

The pressures on you will be different, too, depending on your sex and your parent's. As a daughter, you may be expected to take on traditional female tasks of shopping, cooking, caring for other people. As a son, you may find you have to take responsibility for decisions and practical tasks. Your mother may turn to you for the support she previously got from her husband.

Stepping into your dead parent's shoes is often an unconscious action, and you realize only much later what has happened. For a while it can seem to minimize the pain of your loss by minimizing the impact of your parent's absence. Ultimately, however, it cannot protect you from the impact of the death. The gap left in your life has to be faced at some point and 'being' your parent cannot prevent the pain, it can only, at best, delay it.

• Losing the living parent

On top of losing the parent who dies, one of the biggest changes you have to face is the change that takes place in the remaining parent. Often you may feel you have lost not only the dead parent but the living one as well. This can happen in various ways: either because of the surviving parent's own grief; or because he or she had not taken much of the load of parenting before and this now becomes obvious to you; or because he or she remarries and becomes involved in a new life with a new partner from which you feel excluded.

Sometimes the remaining parent is so changed by grief that the person you knew is changed irrevocably. There may be profound physical change, such as loss or gain of weight, or loss of interest in appearance. This can be extremely distressing to witness. A formerly elegant mother can suddenly become a bedraggled, defeated old woman. A father who was a pillar of respectability can sit in front of the TV all day. It is not at all uncommon for parents to revert to adolescent or even childish behaviour after a bereavement, becoming irritable, unreliable, sullen and remote.

Julian hated watching his father become increasingly adolescent after his mother's death. He needed his father to be strong and reassuring and reliable. Instead he watched in dismay as his father degenerated into an overgrown teenager – slumped in front of the television, living on take-aways, filling the house with empty cans. 'He never drank beer at home before, let alone from cans,' Julian said, genuinely appalled by the change in his father. 'I have to go round picking them up, nagging him to turn the TV off.'

Even when the change is not so dramatic outwardly, you may sense an inner change that is equally alarming and distressing. To see parents vulnerable, hurt and helpless is very frightening, particularly if you have never before had cause to question their solid dependability, their emotional strength and their control over the world, yours in particular. You may have had plenty of cause to criticize them, you may have fought against their attitudes, values, opinions, politics and sexual morality, neverthless they were still unquestionably there for you if you wanted them.

Seeing, or becoming aware, of your mother or father as an individual like yourself, capable of fear, sorrow, pain, and no more able to control the world than you, can shake your entire sense of the way things are. It is like being thrown to the ground by a second earthquake only moments after the first has devastated everything about you. Not only have you lost one parent, you now find you have lost two: the remaining parent is not the person you knew before; he or she may seem self-absorbed, is not available for you to run to, cannot understand your feelings, is perhaps not even interested in your feelings. You may find that suddenly *you* are the parent, you are the one taking responsibility for meals, bills, other siblings, while your so-called parent is like another child about the place: hopeless, helpless, dependent on you.

After my step-father died my mother became very

dependent on me for a while. Normally an independent, determined and implacable woman, who got her children out of bed several hours earlier than we thought civilized, packed us off to music courses and activity weekends, organized us from one minute to the next, she was now suddenly and horribly transformed into someone who simply sat and stared and wept. I had to help her choose what clothes to wear, encourage her to eat, be a shoulder for her to cry on. She would come to me for help with the most straightforward tasks. It appalled me. I hated her being dependent on me. It made it difficult for me to grieve when I was so taken up with caring for her. There was no room or time for my own sorrow. Partly that was a relief: looking after my mother became a convenient excuse to avoid my own painful feelings, but partly it was a great strain. She felt closer to me than before, she said, but I felt completely alienated from her. Who was this woman? I did not know her, I did not like her, she *scared* me. I wrote in my diary at that time:

Mum's dependence leaves me cold. She is like a child, unaware, incapable of nearly everything and always needing care and support and encouragement. The sight of her so weak and vulnerable frightens me, makes me back off emotionally. She often says how glad she is that we are close, that I am the only one who can understand how she feels, but I don't feel close at all. I hate her dependency. I find it revolting. I can't talk to her. I don't want her emotion. But I feel guilty because I should be helping her if I can. I can't talk to her anymore. There is no one in the world for me to talk to now. I can't go to her and tell her how desperate I feel. She is the most dear person in the world to me and I try not to shut her up or out, but her needing me frightens me so much.

I was totally unprepared for my mother's frailty and weakness. I had no place for it in my idea of her. She was strong, independent, unflappable – or had been. Now that she was none of these things, I barely knew her. My father had died, my step-father had died, now it seemed I had lost my mother too.

As the weeks and months passed, she recovered her drive and determination. It was a tremendous relief to me when, a couple of months later, I was able to write:

There are children playing a ball-game outside my window, shrieking with delight every time the ball goes bouncing into the mint patch, sending up a delicious waft of minty air. But best of all, I can hear Mum being efficient and competent downstairs in the kitchen, organizing the washing-up, goading Ellen into playing her violin. It is such a relief to be able to treat Mum like a person again.

But what I really meant was that it was a relief to treat her like a *mother* again. Despite her recovery I still felt that our relationship had changed and that there was a new distance between us. I was wary of her possible demands and held her at arms' length. I also did not feel able to go to her with my problems, aware that she had so many of her own. I was often intolerant and unkind to her, I think perhaps to punish her for no longer being there for me, and although at times I felt overcome with remorse for being so unkind and intolerant, for not being more understanding of what she was going through, I never felt those things quite strongly enough to stop myself. Somewhere inside I was horrified and furious that she was preventing me from being dependent, needy, scared and weak, by being those things herself. As a parent, I thought, she was not supposed to be those things. Everything was topsy-turvy, all skew-whiff, all wrong.

Even after my mother had come to terms with her grief and

I, more or less, with my own, I found it hard to overcome this feeling of having lost her too when my father and step-father died. I had seen her as a fallible human being, and with that insight came a new relationship, perhaps a more equal one in some ways, but not one which usually exists between a child and a mother. That person I had lost, as surely as I had lost my father and step-father. I could never have back the all-supportive, all-encircling, all-protective mother of my childhood – a mother who was in any case perhaps more fantasy than past reality – and I grieved for that loss bitterly and for many years. I did not want to be hauled into an adult world with adult perceptions of things and people, and with cold adult drafts howling in my ears. I did not want to know about death or the weakness of the flesh or the tiny frail thread that binds us to life or how suddenly a heart can stop beating. I did not want to know about choice and responsibility for myself and powerlessness. Wasn't there anywhere to be a child still? The answer I gradually had to accept was, No. It was a bitter discovery.

• Reassessing the living parent

Sometimes after one parent dies, you can realize that you had *already* lost the surviving parent. The parent who has died was actually the one doing *all* the parenting for you. At the very time of your greatest need, death has shone a harsh and unyielding light on the fact that the remaining parent had never really been there for you.

Charlotte was twenty-three when her father died suddenly of a heart attack. A year after his death, Charlotte was depressed, work was going badly and she was often taking days off and staying at home in bed. She avoided company except for very close friends. She could see nothing worthwhile in her life, nor any room for improvement. She thought her depression, and her other problems, might be connected with her father's death, but knowing this was no comfort, because his death was the worst of it all. The problem was not only accepting her father's death, but also having to face up to the parent her mother was not.

Charlotte adored her father and he adored her. He was all-important in her life. Her confidence and encouragement and love came from him. He praised her, encouraged her, advised her, supported her, made her feel worthwhile and important. He made her feel like a significant being in the world. Her mother, by contrast, had always been critical, hostile towards Charlotte's friends, jealous of Charlotte's relationship with her father, ungenerous emotionally, and psychologically unsupportive. After her husband's death, she relied heavily on Charlotte, but was no nicer to her. If anything she became even more carping and critical than before.

Nevertheless Charlotte felt responsible for her mother now that her father was dead. At a time when she needed to protect herself from criticism, to be with people who would be nurturing and gentle with her, she in fact spent more and more time with her mother, who profoundly and persistently undermined her confidence and exaggerated her feelings of worthlessness and uselessness. Spending time with her mother only intensified her longing for her father; the painful presence of the former only spotlighted the painful absence of the latter, aggravating her sense of having lost her friend, comforter, supporter, encourager.

All her mother's criticism confirmed a picture of herself as 'bad' that Charlotte had held inside from early childhood. Until her father's death, his 'good' image of her and her mother's 'bad' image had battled it out, and her father's had won. Now Charlotte had to fight for herself but, grief-stricken, was in no fit state to fight. Instead she tried to make friends with the enemy, unable to realize and accept that there was no real possibility for friendship there. The continual blame she received whenever she saw or spoke with her mother after her father's death was especially wounding when she herself was unarmed and vulnerable. To accept that her mother could in no way make up for her father's absence was intolerably upsetting. Not only was Charlotte having to recognize the enormous importance of her father in her life and her vast need for him, she was also having to recognize how destructive her mother was, and what a negative influence she had always been.

For people who are older when a parent dies, who by then have their own families and their own lives, there will have been time to recognize and adjust to these realizations, to see the fallibility of your parents as people and as parents. With time most people will come to accept the shortcomings of their parents. If they are lucky they also come to see their parent's achievements more clearly too. But there is a proper time and place for these changes and just when one of them has died is not the ideal situation for a reappraisal of your parents. How much easier to do so when you have your own life, independent of your family, your own home, a job, a whole new set of friends, a husband or wife and maybe children of your own. It can seem so unfair, so premature, so inconvenient to have to deal with a parent's death now. And how are you to find the energy and the emotional reserves to deal with these issues when you are drained, drained, drained by the effort of making some sense of death itself?

For Charlotte, as for many people, the death of one parent is not only dreadful in itself, but can often turn out to be the icing on a massive cake of loss.

Sometimes, however, the realization that you have an unsatisfactory or non-existent relationship with the remaining parent can prompt more positive changes.

Kate was also forced to reappraise her relationship with the remaining parent, but for her the outcome was much happier. Her mother died when she was twenty-one and she quickly realized just how little she knew her father and just how little he had done as a father. 'He was the kind of father,' she says, 'who'd come in from work, pat his children on the head on the way through the living-room, and disappear into his study for the rest of the evening. We didn't know him at all. We never saw him. He never spoke to us.' When her father took to saying to Kate and her sisters, 'You wish it had been me, don't you?' they knew there was some truth in his words. But six years on Kate can say unequivocally that she is glad her father did not die because her mother's death forced them to get to know each other. 'I would never have known him otherwise, and now we have a real relationship and I'm very glad about that.'

But their relationship is not a traditional daughter-father one: Kate is not unusual in finding that, in a curious way, her father stopped being a parent in the way he had been before his wife died. Instead he became something closer to a friend or sibling. One immediate and significant change was that Kate's father stopped referring to his wife as 'Mummy' and began to use her Christian name. He also began to talk about

Kate's mother as a person, someone he had loved and lived and argued with. His elevated role of parent, of father, vanished when the partner in his double act died. 'Dad started to talk about her in a way he never had before,' Kate recalls. 'He was much more open about their relationship, talked to us as if we were friends not daughters. At first I felt uneasy about it and resented that he wasn't doing more to look after us, but I've accepted it now.'

This kind of change is not so surprising when you consider that your parents may have presented themselves to you as parents, but to each other they were still two people who had once fallen in love and chosen to spend their lives together for better or worse. After one of them dies, it is that role that seems most significant to the remaining partner: the role of companion, supporter, partner and lover. A grieving father becomes first and foremost a grieving man; similarly a grieving mother becomes a woman who has lost her mate. What you lose is both parents.

• Losing a parent through marriage

A third way in which the death of one parent can lead to the loss of the remaining parent is through remarriage. Whether this happens three months after the funeral or three years after, it can be far more difficult to cope with than other people suppose. But it is certainly not uncommon for the remaining parent to remarry, particularly not for men, who are statistically far more likely to remarry than women. It is also not uncommon for people to remarry within a relatively short space of time: in an Australian study of 126 widows and widowers, all those who remarried did so within 12-18 months of their spouse's death.

There are many reasons why men are more likely to remarry than women, but usually they do so for pragmatic reasons. Perhaps your parents' marriage was organized along very traditional lines and your father simply cannot look after himself on a day-to-day basis, feels overwhelmed by the business of washing clothes, shopping and cooking. Fathers are – still – often unable to cope with their children's needs and may welcome a woman to help with them. In *Coping With Grief* Susan Wallbank suggests that there may be a connection between the high incidence of men remarrying and the fact that society discourages men from showing their emotions. This makes them far less likely than women to share their sorrow and their worries with friends, and more likely to form close attachments to new partners who can empathize and sympathize with what they are going through. In many cases men not only rely on women to share their feelings, but actually let women have the emotions for them. After the death of a partner, the need for emotional and physical closeness can be very great and it is certainly harder in Western society for men to find that solace from friends and relatives than it is for women to do so.

Whatever the reasons and whatever the timing, remarriage can be surprisingly hard to cope with. It may leave you with an acute sence of betrayal, may seem to deny the existence of the parent who died, may seem to reduce him or her to total insignificance. You may well feel considerable anger towards your remarrying parent. There seem to be so many unacceptable thoughts: 'It's all right for Mum to have someone to comfort her, but what about someone to comfort me?' There is the voice that says, 'So how much did Dad really love Mum if he has found someone new so soon?' There is the awful feeling that your dead parent is going to be replaced somehow, and nagging concerns that you will be expected to love this person, call them Mum or Dad, or have to be told what to do by this stranger in your home. You may well draw comparisons between the new partner and your dead parent. You may well feel that the parent you had relied on for love and support has abandoned you, has withdrawn, wrapped up in this new relationship with no time or feeling or concern left over for you. Even if you were close, it can feel as if a wall has sprung up between you and your parent. They are always busy, never there when you need them, your requirements have to take second place because of the new person in their life. On top of the hurtfulness of all that, there is often a sense of disgust, repugnance: 'How could they? How could they be happy again, so soon?' Realizing that parents can be weak, fearful and vulnerable, often feels like an additional loss, and in the same way so can realizing that they are sexual beings who need physical affection, feel desire and are desirable. In *Hamlet* this revulsion and betrayal which a child can feel when one parent dies and the other remarries is powerfully evoked. Hamlet rages about his mother:

> . . . within a month,
> Ere yet the salt of most unrighteous tears
> Had left the flushing in her galled eyes,
> She married. O! most wicked speed . . . .

He makes the common mistake of the young in thinking older people incapable of sexual desire: 'You cannot call it love,' he says to her, 'for at your age the hey-day in the blood is tame.' He is disgusted, enraged, outraged and bewildered by the fact that she is now not only a mother to him, but a woman acting on her own needs and desires as a sexual being. Hamlet is an extreme case, perhaps, but many of these feelings are there in lesser forms when a parent remarries.

When my mother remarried last year, I oohed and aahed sincerely enough at the photographs of her wedding day, but I could not quite cope with the one of her and her new husband kissing on the mouth. In fact I found the whole business of my mother being in love pretty hard to handle. At her age! Now I am calmer about her remarriage and can regard my own reaction with a degree of amusement. But at the time I was very distressed and frequently burst into tears without really understanding why. In the worst moments I felt as if I were in the Terry Gilliam film, 'Brazil' in which the mother of the main character really does get younger instead of older. One day he turns up at her house in desperate trouble, needing her help, and finds her surrounded by adoring lovers, all about half his age. 'Not now,' she says, 'I'm busy.'

After her mother died of cancer, Sue experienced all three ways of losing a living parent: she felt she lost her father first of all through his grief, then through her own reappraisal of their relationship, and finally through his remarriage.

Sue's mother died when she was eighteen and within a few months Sue's father fell in love with a friend of the family and decided to remarry. The woman was also widowed and had two children by her previous marriage. Not only did Sue have a 'new mother' to cope with – and of course this 'new' father – she also had a new set of siblings. In the next couple of years Sue became moody and easily disheartened when things went wrong. She left university, started to do a design course but dropped out after a week, decided to travel round the world, but somehow ended up working as a secretary for a local firm and living at home. She also started to have a series of relationships, all of which began very intensely and ended very rapidly. Furthermore, all her relationships seemed to happen simultaneously, as if she were incapable of committing herself to any one person at any one time. Sue did not at all enjoy the complications and deception this habitual two-timing involved, but she found it impossible to break the pattern.

It was as if she herself were split in two: there was the part of herself that was pleased for her father and the part that was angry and disappointed with him. There was the part of her that liked her step-mother and the part that hated her for usurping her mother. She partly liked having a new brother and sister, but partly hated the intrusion of these strangers into her life. There was the part of her that also wanted, like her father, to be able to forget the pain of her mother's death and fall in love and be healed, but there was a part of her that wanted to keep her mother alive by not entering into life and love again. She was divided within herself, by split loyalties to her father and to her mother, and by split ideas about how life should proceed after her mother's death.

Distracted and vague at the best of times, Sue's father was even more so now, in the throes of both grief and new love. Not by any means an unkind man, he simply did not notice what his daughter was up to, and if he did, he put it down to her age and the death of his wife.

Her predicament was like that of the man in Stevie Smith's poem, *Not waving but drowning*:

> Nobody heard him, the dead man,
> But still he lay moaning:

I was much further out than you thought
And not waving but drowning.

Poor chap, he always loved larking
And now he's dead
It must have been too cold for him his heart gave way,
They said.

Oh, no no no, it was too cold always
(Still the dead one lay moaning)
I was much too far out all my life
And not waving but drowning.'

Sue lost her father through remarriage and she lost him because he was not there in her life as she needed him to be. It was several years before she accepted that he could never replace her mother in the sense of being an active, guiding presence, and until she began to accept that she was trapped by her anger with him for having 'disappeared' when she so needed him, and trapped into self-destructive behaviour by her confusion and hidden need both for support and revenge.

Losing the living parent is a lot to take on board at a time when the boat you are on already feels pretty shaky. You may find yourself feeling resentful or angry as a result, either towards your remaining parent or towards the one who has died. You may feel they have failed to look after you, failed to protect you from the harshness of the world; that by dying or remarrying, or simply by being grief-stricken themselves, they have let you down badly. You may hate your dead parent for dying and leaving the family with so many problems to sort out alone. You may hate the living parent for failing to sort out these problems.

It takes time to understand how you are affected by these changes and time to get used to the changes themselves. Every change involves loss and every loss is hard to handle right now. In the meantime, try to be gentle with yourself. Rather than beating your head against the brick wall of a parent's absence, physical or emotional, save your energy for the more useful task of caring for yourself.

● Losing your faith

People generally assume that religious faith will help you through difficult times in your life, but you may in fact find that your religious faith is no help at all. On the contrary, you may feel that it is failing you just when you need it most, and that your parent's death makes a mockery of faith in God. You may ask yourself: how can there be a just God when this has happened. You may feel that your sorrow and pain proves there cannot be a caring God.

The sensation of having been let down by God and by your faith at the same time that so much else that was solid in your life seems to be collapsing can be the cause of great despair and anguish. It is as if there is nothing left to hang on to any more, no source of hope, no core of goodness. To lose your faith on top of everything can add considerably to your feelings of hopelessness and pointlessness. If your faith is important to you, it may be worth finding someone with whom you can discuss your feelings and doubts. One rabbi I spoke to about the additional stress caused by loss of faith after a parent's death suggested: 'If there is anger at God, tell him. Tell him that you feel cheated and let down. It is important to be angry.'

But once you have done that, he said, you should take a look at your expectations of life and of God. 'Religion is there not to stop awful things happening, but to help you when they do happen. God is not a divine vending machine where you put in your coin and get out what you want. God is someone to turn to, to help you deal with life as it is, not to change it.'

Different religions will have different approaches to the feelings of the bereaved. It is important to hang on to the fact that your feelings of anger have their place – religious faith worth having will make room for that anger, not deny it.

• Losing your base

When things are changing fast in your life, you need a still point of reference, a place or situation which remains the same, solid and dependable; somewhere you can come back to, despise for being boring and staid, if you want, and then return with confidence to your new and more exciting life, your batteries recharged.

Unfortunately, it is precisely this still point of reference that is often missing after a parent's death.

My step-father died while I was at university and I found it very difficult that the firm base of my home was not there for me. I went away each term and came back in the holidays to find the people and places I had left behind more changed than the one I had gone away to. I needed stability, but it was no longer to be found at home. Rooms were rearranged; furniture sold; books and possessions boxed up or thrown away. My mother was distracted, anxious, frantically overworked. My little brother and sister mothered her. It was all very strange and bewildering.

159

Other friends who were also trying to adjust after a bereavement were having the same difficulty: their need for a secure base to return to, in order to be with people who understood them, was frustrated, because 'home' was where most of the change was taking place.

Maria could not stand the feeling of being totally adrift. In her first term at university she was surrounded by new people and places. At home everything had changed radically since her mother's death. She so hated feeling that while she was away her home – such as it was now – was disappearing altogether, that she decided to take a year off and went back home to be with her father and sister. At least there she could see what was changing, rather than being abruptly confronted with the change when she came home in the holidays.

Carina, on the other hand, decided to go to college as planned. Her father had died very recently and the start of her first term coincided with the rest of her family deciding to move to another part of the country. She felt very isolated at college, so far from her family, but she was determined to stick it out. Years later she realized how hard it had been for her to have all these changes taking place simultaneously, but at the time Carina focused all her energy on the need to 'settle down' at college, make friends, fit in. She was often confused by how difficult she was finding it, but didn't relate these difficulties to all the huge changes in her life. For Carina, the easiest option was to make college the firm base, and that was what she worked to create.

• Losing possessions

The sense that your life is no longer based on firm

foundations, that once-familiar people and places have become strange to you, is often accentuated by the loss of actual *things*. When so much in your life is in flux it is not at all uncommon to attach enormous importance to personal possessions. In a brooch or a book or a photograph you can find at least something that remains unchanged. The business of disposing of your dead parent's belongings can therefore be extremely fraught and upsetting. Where there isn't a will, this can sometimes make the division of possessions and property a lengthy process, which may add considerably to the distress it causes you and your family.

The ultimate say over what happens to possessions will usually be in the hands of your remaining parent or lawyers. This can exacerbate the feeling of being powerless, the feeling that your relationship with the parent who has died will not be valued by others.

Immediately after my father's death I was obsessed with the need to have things of his to remind me of him, to keep him alive in some way. I wanted to build a fortress of his books and clothes and pictures, and hide inside it. I needed his things to make me feel he was still there with me. I was panicky with the fear that he would just slip away, vanish totally, that there would be no trace of him left behind. I was anxious lest my step-mother failed to realize how important my father's belongings were to me, anxious lest other brothers and sisters took things I felt I needed.

It is not at all unusual after a death for people to react very strongly to the question of the dead person's belongings. Sometimes people are very reluctant to move anything at all. Occasionally this reluctance gets out of hand and people create a sort of shrine to the dead person's memory, at which they then worship. The sad irony of this is that the memory they are so frantic to keep alive is rarely the memory of the real live flesh-and-blood good-and-bad person who lived.

Sometimes the opposite happens: a widowed husband or wife will want to destroy, burn or throw out all evidence of the dead person, as if the pain occasioned by the presence of these belongings is simply too much to bear. If you do not feel the same way, this apparent desire to annihilate your dead mother or father's existence can be very painful, and will require you to look very carefully at the underlying motives for your living parent's actions: perhaps it is a way of expressing anger or a way of punishing themselves for 'allowing' their partner to die; perhaps it is motivated by a powerful fear that they will never 'get over it' and must therefore get a grip, get on with life, not 'give in' to grief in any way at all.

While you can try to accept your parent's need to do things in a particular way, at the same time do recognize the importance of your own needs. You may not be able to prevent your parent getting rid of belongings before you would want, but you can perhaps find a memento that you can keep.

Sometimes, however, the remaining parent will give you responsibility for getting rid of your dead parent's belongings. Think carefully how you want to do this: should a collection of books be kept intact and given to a local library? Would a set of records make a good present to a school or hospital? Clothes can be thrown away or given to charity. If you are in need of extra money, clothes, books and records can all be sold to second-hand shops.

If you do not feel up to the task right after the funeral, then leave it until you do. There is no particular rush. You may feel pressure to get everything back to normal as quickly as possible, but in reality you will find that it is a long time before that happens and the speed with which you dispose of possessions is not the determining factor. Most people find the time announces itself when it is right to do this painful kind of clearing out. Don't feel you must hurry up and decide. Out of sight is not out of mind and the presence of possessions will neither stop you and your family from feeling miserable, nor will possessions disposed of magically make you all feel better.

Give yourself enough time in disposing of the main belongings to be ready to do so. When the time does come, it can be useful to get a friend to help as the presence of someone who is not emotionally bound up with these belongings can help you to think more calmly and clearly about what to do with them. Similarly give yourself all the time you need to find what token or memento you want to keep with you. Some things you will want to have around for many years to come, others you may only need to have for a few months. My younger sister has a locket that she wears with a photograph of her father inside. A friend has a skirt of her mother's, another has his Dad's football scarf.

● Losing your memories

Even when you yourself have decided to throw things away, losing things can be hard. One of the reasons why it can be so distressing is because possessions are often intimately bound up with memories, and memories are precious and fragile to you now. There is often a real fear that once the clothes and books and records have been given away or you have left the

163

home where you and your parent lived, you will no longer be able to remember your parent properly, that the death will somehow happen all over again in the failure of your memory.

When his father died, Alan sat in his bedroom and every single thing around him reminded him of his father. When a few years later his mother remarried and the house was reorganized to accommodate her new husband, Alan moved to a different room in the house. Dismantling his bedroom was excruciatingly painful, because in his mind it was so bound up with his father: these triggers of photographs, books and ornaments had helped keep his father alive for him.

If for whatever reason you are not able to keep belongings that mean a lot to you, then at least allow yourself to think about what the object really represents for you: does it remind you of your parent's sense of humour or some other lovable and particular characteristic? If you can focus on the specific value and significance of the object that is lost, you may well find that the memory of the cherished aspect of your mother or father is still with you.

Memories are important and you are entitled to them. One of the hardest aspects of life without a parent is the nagging feeling that you ought really to stop remembering them, that memories are rather self-indulgent and generally a sign of weakness.

I still have a jumper of my father's that has long been too full of holes actually to be worn, but I cannot quite bring myself to throw it away. Apart from the jumper and a photograph, I have few physical reminders of him. Over the years I have honed down the mementoes and memory joggers, the physical signs of my father, but I have done so very gradually, almost without noticing, letting go of things as I no longer feel the need for them; along with this has come, also gradually, a slowly increasing confidence that my father is alive in my memory, that he will not fade away to nothing. I know now, though no one could have told me this, that the memory is solid, unshakeable, sometimes more powerful, sometimes less so, but always there. I don't have access to memories of every single moment we ever spent together, but over the years the familiar memories come and go and I have found myself remembering new things too.

The only way my father could cease to be would be if I died myself. The very fact that I exist reminds me of him. I am here because of him, my existence is proof of his existence and a constant reminder of him – sometimes comfortingly, sometimes less so. As long as I live, so he lives in me, in my memories of him and in the part of me that is him. I have heard other people say this too. Annie expressed it perfectly when she said about her father's death: 'Only half of that relationship died, the part of it that was him. The other half, the half that is me, is still alive.'

Memories are a vital way of keeping someone alive. In parts of Africa, some tribal people do not regard eternity as something that exists in the future, instead they see eternity as stretching out *behind* them, and when they die they join, in their turn, the eternal beings who live forever in the flesh and in the memories of the living. Each new generation keeps alive the previous one through memory. Nomadic people attach great importance to the past. When you can't locate yourself in time by a specific place, the sense of continuity must come through attention to who your ancestors were. You learn where you come from in terms of people rather than places: lineage becomes very important.

When recently I took a friend to a Jewish wedding, he was astonished by the speeches: 'It's like something out of the Old Testament,' he said afterwards, referring to the way each speaker in turn had emphasized the ancestry of the bride and groom, mentioning by name maternal and paternal grandparents, great-grandparents, great-great-grandparents. This long recitation of names and the powerful invocation of the past was not something he had come across before, but it served a useful purpose: it secured the new couple in the present, placed them firmly in the context of the past, and gave them a solid base from which to launch themselves into the uncertainties of the future. It is by using memory in this way that you keep the past alive. This is not the same as trying to pretend the dead are not dead, but rather a gift that enables you to keep alive the importance to you of those who are dead.

7 Changes and losses – the public kind

'One change leaves the way open
for the introduction of others.'
(Machiavelli)

The changes and losses described so far are ones that may well be painfully obvious to you without being very apparent to people beyond your immediate family. They are changes and losses that you have to cope with privately, with relatively little support. Other changes in your life, however, will be more noticeable to the outside world. Moving house, changing jobs, ending a relationship: these kinds of change are not specifically related to a bereavement and are not considered at all out of the ordinary. As changes, they will be generally recognized, but as losses, which for you they are also, the significance of these events may be entirely lost on other people. For this reason, these 'ordinary' changes and losses can be just as hard to bear.

• Losing your home

Moving house is always an upheaval and unfortunately a

parent's death often makes such a move unavoidable. Moving house, however, is more than a time- and energy-consuming nuisance: it is an event which can arouse intensely painful feelings. If possessions are bound up with memories, how much more so are places.

In *The Trauma of Moving*, Audrey T. McCollum describes how even at the best of times moving can be upsetting. Her book is primarily a psychology text-book about the effects on women of moving, but her conclusions have a wider relevance. She quotes one of her interviewees as saying: 'Moving is like dying. I felt at one with my home. I was afraid of losing it, of feeling alone. It's like dying, because dying means aloneness.'

Summing up, McCollum states that:

Moving meant experiencing psychological homelessness ... an interruption of the sense of continuity, and a loss of feelings of mastery. This limbo kindles anxiety in the present and rekindled anxiety from the past ... Moving meant enduring disorientation, confusion, disorganization – a loss of control, a temporary loss of the sense of competence that is a foundation of self-esteem.

When it comes on top of other losses, moving home can be particularly distressing. The re-location of your physical belongings and self means dis-location from where you were before. Unless you feel very secure and steady inside yourself, which is highly unlikely in the circumstances, that dislocation will probably be extremely painful. You are losing part of yourself, the part of you that lived in that home, the connection with things that happened while you lived there, and the connection with the people and possessions you lived there with. Places keep memories alive. Going back to a place invariably stirs memories and leaving a place invariably stirs them too. It stirs a sense of the past slipping away.

168

After a parent's death it is unfortunately often necessary to move house, whether because of shortage of money, or a need for the remaining parent to be closer to work, relatives or schools. But to lose your home, the familiarity of your surroundings, at a time when everything feels so strange and fragile is hard. It can feel as if nothing is left untouched by this death. It is reaching out and spoiling every aspect of your life. The process of dismantling your home and packing up belongings can feel extremely destructive, especially at a time when so much in your life seems to be falling apart.

Accepting that packing and moving are always traumatic makes it easier to accept that when you are already sensitized to loss, separation and instability, they will be especially so. Your reactions are not abnormal: to feel nothing at such a time would in fact be stranger.

● Losing your job

When Michael left his job in a publishing company, a job he had never enjoyed, to set up in business as a furniture maker, he failed to realize that this change would involve loss. He expected to be relieved, liberated and full of zeal for his new life. Instead he became depressed, listless and lacking in confidence. Four years earlier his mother had died of multiple sclerosis and as his change of job came fairly soon after the tragedy of her death, he was less able to cope than he might have been with the losses that this new change entailed. And even though it was a change he had chosen and wanted to make, it involved substantial loss. For example, Michael suddenly found himself without company during the day, without the structure of an office, without anyone to have lunch with, gossip with or make coffee for. There was no one to care or notice whether he got up in the morning or what he wore, let alone whether he did one stroke of work or not.

Michael also suffered from two other significant losses when he left his job: he lost part of his identity, the part that was a book editor and worked in a smart office in central London, and he also lost the sense of someone else being responsible for his welfare. These losses in particular were disturbing because they echoed similar losses he had felt after his mother's death: then too he had felt very keenly the loss of identity and the loss of someone who had been responsible for him. Being only half aware of these similarities complicated matters further. Not understanding why he was coping so badly with something he had wanted to do – leave a job he wasn't enjoying – made it worse. He felt all the bewilderment and self-doubt that had besieged him after his mother's death, but could not understand why.

If he could have anticipated the similarities, expected the present losses to reactivate memories of the previous losses, Michael might have been spared some of the shock and sense of failure. He could have allowed himself an adjustment phase, in which to grieve for what he was losing by leaving his job, instead of just expecting to be full of energy and enthusiasm for his new life, and being angry and disappointed with himself for not being.

Michael's loss was one he had a certain degree of control over since he decided to leave his job, but often you will not have control of changes and losses in your life: redundancy, for example, can be extremely painful. However it happens, the loss of professional identity is hard to cope with (it is no coincidence that a large proportion of men die within three years of retirement), and when it comes on top of a bereavement this additional loss can be excruciating.

Jim was twenty-one when his father died after a long and difficult illness. He and Jim had had a complicated relationship and Jim felt guilty after his father's death that he had not been a 'better' son. He also felt bad that he had not been around more in his father's illness and that he was not spending more time now with his widowed mother. A few months after his father died, Jim lost his job in the local theatre where he ran the foyer bar. This second loss in such a short time was too much. He became unable to do anything but sleep and watch television. Very depressed by now, he stopped going out, stopped looking for jobs, stopped talking to his girlfriend or other friends.

For Jim the loss of this job was particularly hard to cope with because it was an area of strife between his father and him. His father had complained that Jim didn't have a proper job and was not taking work seriously enough. Jim always felt his father regarded him as a failure professionally, but had hoped he would be proud of the job in the local theatre. When his father died, Jim felt a tremendous sense of failure. Irrationally he blamed himself for his father's illness and death, and felt guilty about his behaviour before and after his father's death. His job was his one area of self-pride, in which he hoped eventually to win approval from his father, and when he lost the job it compounded and intensified his already profound sense of failure.

● Losing a relationship

A job is not the only thing the loss of which gives rise to

171

powerful feelings. Losing a partner can also be the catalyst for reawakened grief after a bereavement.

Mark was apparently unaffected by his mother's death when he was seventeen. For almost a year, everyone kept saying how well he seemed to have adjusted. Shortly before his mother died he had started going out with Jessica and she had stuck by him, being loving and supportive during the months after his mother's death. People often remarked that Jessica even somewhat resembled Mark's mother. When Jessica finished the relationship after about a year, Mark was completely devastated. All the feelings he had not expressed after his mother died now came out. Jessica had somehow replaced his mother in his mind and heart, and made it possible to avoid grieving for her. When Jessica 'died' too, it released a storm of grief.

As with losing a job or a house, it is vital to recognize what you are losing when a relationship ends and to allow yourself to mourn for it. It is equally vital not to pretend it has no connection with losses in your life that have gone before.

• Happy changes

Sometimes the changes in your life will be happy occasions, such as Christmas or birthdays or weddings. Even so they may still awaken sad memories and painful feelings of loss. A Christmas spent in the absence of one of your parents is bound to be the cause of mixed emotions, however much happiness there also is, simply because the absence will remind you of the death and of previous Christmases when that parent was there. Even happy occasions can involve loss. *Any* event that involves the gain of something new will involve also the loss of something old. Change involves loss, even when it is change that is wanted and joyful, and loss in any circumstances will feel harder right now than it might at a different time in your life.

Marriage is the obvious and most dramatic example, whether it is the marriage of siblings or parents. Why do brides' mothers traditionally weep at weddings? Not just for joy, that's for sure. They are crying also for the loss of their little girls, for the loss of sexual innocence, for the loss of their own prime position in their daughters' lives, and for the loss of their own youth; for the passing of time and with it their own lives. Similarly the birth of a child is often accompanied by self-doubt and depression in the new mother, not purely because of lack of sleep. It is also because of the loss of identity, perhaps the loss of a youthful figure, the loss of carefreeness.

Change means loss as well as gain, and loss may hurt.

On the day of my brother's wedding, I cried all morning. I was thrilled for him and thought my future sister-in-law was great. But for me it felt like I was losing my brother, as I had lost my father. For an hour or so it felt like a tragedy!

Will is marrying in the autumn. He can't understand why his mother and sister aren't unequivocally delighted. He is cross and rather hurt that they are less than over-the-moon. His sister explains, 'It's not that we're not pleased and we think she is lovely. But it's a sad time of year anyway, the time of year when our father died. And since he died we've been quite dependent on each other. Now it's like Will won't be needing us any more. It feels a bit like we're losing him too.'

In the months leading up to my own marriage I was very

173

aware that there would be moments of sadness in the wedding day for me and my family because my father and step-father would not be there. I would have liked them to have met my husband, and I would have liked them to have been there sharing the celebrations with us. I knew beforehand that I would miss their presence, and at the risk of casting a damper on the occasion I decided to ask an old family friend to make the speech traditionally made by the bride's father, and in his speech to mention my father and step-father, so that through a moment of mentioning them and remembering them they would be there. On the day the friend made the speech and spoke with affection and respect about my father and step-father. This explicit reference to death and sorrow in the context of so much happiness was very moving for me, and no one found it distasteful. On the contrary, the celebration of life and love that lies at the very heart of a wedding was somehow deepened, not diminished, by the honest acceptance that loss and grief are also a part of marriage. Above all I was left feeling that two people who had had everything to do with bringing me to that point in time, my wedding day, had been included in the festivities, publicly welcomed in to join the party, so that their faces too had been amongst the many smiling faces that day.

In parts of rural Greece laments are sung at weddings in recognition of the loss involved in marriage as well as the joy. Making a place for sadness in this way is very helpful, though rare. Occasions and events that the outside world regards as joyous, but which for you may be painful and difficult, can be extremely upsetting. After a parent's death these 'joyous' events are usually ambivalent at best, and at worst, they can be appalling. Christmas, birthdays, anniversaries and weddings are all times when your sense of loss may be reawakened: everyone else wants to celebrate but you feel miserable. The important thing is not to deny what you are feeling, but to acknowledge to yourself that it is right and proper in the circumstances. Sometimes it can be a great relief to make this acknowledgement public, perhaps by lighting a candle in remembrance of your parent or saying a short prayer or reading a poem. Recognition of sad feelings need not be depressing, instead it can actually make it easier to enjoy the joyful aspects of a celebration. Far more depressing is having to pretend to be enjoying yourself when you're not.

● Losing your youth

Perhaps the greatest and most traumatic loss after a parent's death is the loss of your youth. Having to 'grow up overnight' is one of the most common and often difficult experiences when a parent dies at an early age. Responsibilities come suddenly and these external pressures can accentuate the inner feeling that your youth is over.

People often said to me after my father died, 'Well, at least you're young. Young people are more resilient.' Perhaps that is true, I don't know; what I do know is how unhelpful and how hurtful I found that comment. Because the other side of being young when a parent dies is that you are not so ready for it, you have fewer resources for dealing with it, and you are less supported afterwards. Friends, however well-meaning, are often unable to help simply because they do not really know what you are going through. They do not know and cannot guess how long you go on feeling miserable and lost and directionless, how long you go on missing your parent. Relatives and friends of the family often make the same mistake, thinking that because you are young, you will 'get over it' quickly.

I was lucky in knowing a couple who had been close friends of my father. They did not try to sweep my feelings under the carpet. The husband had been through the death of his own father at the age of fourteen and understood very well what I was going through. I often used to go and spend a couple of hours with them at weekends, and they were the only people who really just let me sit and be miserable and miss Dad without feeling ashamed of not having 'got over it by now'. I am still very grateful for their understanding and their help in keeping him alive in memory – not conspiring to kill his existence and importance to me through silence, as so many others do out of a combination of ignorance, insensitivity and embarrassment.

When you are young, death comes as more of an outrage, more of a shock than when you are older. At eighteen, twenty or twenty-four you have barely admitted to yourself that death is real. You may have read books or seen films in which the hero dies and been moved by it; you may have written poems and stories about death; you may have lain in bed at night fantasizing about being orphaned and how terrible it would be. You may well have wished your parents dead on occasion. But it is still the *very last thing* you actually expect to happen. Death is not yet part of your experience nor part of the framework of your life.

What makes coping with death so hard at this age is that even after it *has* become real to you, even while you are struggling with the full horror of it, your friends continue as before. What other people often cannot comprehend is that in some ways you are no longer like other young people. In my experience and the experience of others I have talked to, it is the sense of isolation that makes death particularly hard to cope with at this age. You may well feel isolated from everyone: family, relatives, friends. You are not part of an adult world – in their eyes or yours – yet you no longer belong as before with the younger world of your friends and contemporaries.

When someone you love dies at this stage of your life, you are left in a kind of limbo between youth and adulthood which can be a very lonely, frightening place. The loss of your youth is something also to be mourned.

I was trying to recently describe to a friend how it feels when a parent dies and to explain why it is different at this age than at any other age. I was saying how difficult it becomes after a parent's death to do the very things that everyone else of your age is finding perfectly easy and natural; how you feel pulled in the wrong direction, as if all the momentum of your life has got snarled up. 'Oh, I see,' he said. 'It sounds rather like a train pulling out of a station and gathering speed as it heads out on its journey, but instead it suddenly stops and is shunted back in to the station again.' Yes, I said, that was certainly very close to how I had felt.

Bereavement hit my family in a big way just as I was on my way out of the station. Like my friends I had been preparing for the journey away from home, away from school, away from the city I'd grown up in, away from old places and old friends. I was sorry to be leaving some of these things to be sure, but I was also impatient to be off, excited about the new things ahead, the new people to meet, new things to see, new places

177

to go. We all of us felt a bit precarious perched on the edge of this new life, and we took to reminding each other about the past – Remember the time we blew fairy-liquid bubbles in the maths lesson? Remember how you fancied the history teacher? Remember the time Sally dropped the iron filings and the physics teacher said, 'Just like a girl!'? Remember how we used to go for midnight walks, and the time your boyfriend came to supper and thought the table mat was a plate? Remember the time Helen thought the love-bite on your neck was a bruise and asked how you'd got it?

It was fun, this wallowing in the past, it made the uncertainties of the future less worrying, reminding us that what was to come would be built on top of a good firm base. We were celebrating what had been before and preparing for what was to come next. But then suddenly the future was eclipsed. In the immediate aftermath of my father's death the present and the past took over, shutting out any space for thoughts of anything else. I felt suspended between the enormous task of getting through the existing moment, that day and maybe the next, and toiling with the past, trying to make sense of the present by understanding better how we had got there. There was no room for the awesome prospect of the future, a life without my father, a life full of pain and absence and sorrow.

As time passed the future reasserted itself and, like my friends, I too had to start thinking once more about the life out there waiting for me, the new world I had been preparing to set out towards. And it was still there, as it had been, with the same challenges and opportunities, except that they looked different from where I was now standing. Unlike my friends, I no longer felt that the exciting newness of 'out there' compensated for the loss of the old familiar things 'back here'. A world without my well-known friends and the town I knew and the home I was familiar with seemed to me a frightening, daunting prospect. I didn't much want to get to know new things. The old things seemed strange and unfamiliar enough now. I needed to stay close to whatever was vaguely familiar in the midst of so much strangeness.

I could no longer trust that things or people would be there when I came back. After all, Dad had not been, was the way my logic ran. I no longer felt able to say goodbye to schoolfriends as casually and confidently as they could to me. The loss seemed so much more real to me than anything else, the possible gains to be had out there in the world seemed, conversely, to be like pennies in quicksand and it was too risky even to grab at them.

I hated feeling like this. I hated feeling so much more scared and apprehensive than my friends. I hated feeling different from them. I hated the sensation that I valued them more than they valued me. I hated the doom-and-gloom outlook that I was unable to escape from. I hated not being on my way out of the station with the rest of them. I hated feeling torn between wanting to go too and wanting to stay put, to cling to whatever was stable and familiar in the wreckage and chaos of life-post-death, to avoid at all cost any more loss.

What you lose when a parent dies is the illusion of immortality – yours no less than your parent's. Death shows you like nothing else just how fragile you are, just how insecure is your grasp of the mortal coil, how quickly and easily a life can end, and how totally final it is when that happens. The absoluteness of death is deeply shocking when it first affects your life. Nothing prepares you for it, and nothing reduces the

179

shock of its impact. The world looks different because
suddenly the world *is* different. Your view of the world is quite
different. You no longer view it from the same angle as your
friends because you have experienced an aspect of it that they
have not.

I remember feeling responsible in a curious way for friends,
fearing for their lives as they set off down some country lane
driving far too fast with far too much beer in their blood. They
were excited, having fun: I was terrified. All I could think
about was how dangerous it was, how they ought to be more
careful, how awful it would be for their families if they were
killed. I was always in the back seat saying: 'Could you slow
down a bit . . .'. I felt a degree of responsibility for them that
they certainly did not feel for themselves. I was fearful for their
lives of which they were careless. They still believed in their
own immortality: I knew they were all too mortal. I wanted to
be as happy-go-lucky, as carefree, as fast-living as they, but I
couldn't be, however much I wanted to, because the world
around me felt now an unsafe, risky place, and death all too
real a possiblity. My world *was* an unsafe place, the goalposts
of my life had been radically rearranged, never mind moved:
the pitch had been ploughed up and the posts shredded for
sawdust. It all made me feel very distant from my friends, for
whom nothing had changed.

The losses that come with this stage of life, such as moving
away from home or leaving your schoolfriends, are like losing
parts of yourself. Even if they are parts you quite want to lose, it
is as if you have been scraped so raw that even the smallest
additional loss grates unbearably. You can help yourself
through this painful rite of passage by allowing yourself to be
different. Accept that what seems to others like exciting new

180

gains, feels to you like yet more loss. Accept that you are more sensitive right now than they to that side of things and allow yourself to mourn for what is lost, temporarily as well as permanently. Temporary loss may not be painful to someone else, but it may well be for you. Try not to be too hard on yourself, don't punish yourself for being less courageous, less adventurous, less carefree than other people. You are in a fragile state and you need to treat yourself with care.

• Coping with change and loss

The novelist and broadcaster, Sarah Dunant, once said that finding the right publisher for her books was like finding the right man to marry. She had toyed with the idea of other publishers, made a few advances. But when the real thing came along, she knew it when she saw it. I think it is the same with death. It fascinates you. You long to know how it feels, how it happens, where it starts and ends, so you play around with your life a bit to find out. But once you've had a good big eyeful of death's ugly face, you can recognize it a long way off. And unlike men or publishers, once you have found out what the real thing is, you don't need or want to get unnecessarily close to it *ever* again.

While you are still vulnerable after this shocking sight of death, you will see and feel it in other smaller losses. Do not try and stop yourself feeling the pain of loss. Loss is unavoidable in life and so therefore is pain. The smaller losses provide an opportunity for you to get used to the basic sensation of loss and so become a little more at ease with the weight on your shoulders of the earlier, larger loss of the person you loved.

181

You are not unlike a weight-lifter who knows what tonnage he or she wants to carry, but who trains on lighter weights to begin with, building up strength for the heaviest. Unfortunately the weight of grief is the first to land heavily on your shoulders and *then* you have to lift the slightly lighter ones. On top of the heaviest one of all even they can seem too much, although in themselves they would be bearable. The idea is to find ways of putting down the total burden of loss and instead to take each little one as it comes. You know that the big one is there on the floor beside you all the while, waiting for you, demanding sooner or later to be lifted and borne, but for the meantime you can see how the smaller weights feel. And when you are ready, *then* . . .

Weight management is a useful way of regarding the myriad losses that make up a week, a month, a year. It is not an avoidance technique, simply a way of working with your strength and with your weakness, being realistic about your capabilities. It can be helpful to say to yourself 'OK. This one is too big. It is too much for me right now. I'll put it here for the moment and tackle it in a little while.' Trying to lift everything at once, to bear the whole weight together would be crazy. For others it might not be too much; for you it may be the proverbial straw that breaks the camel's back. Be easy on yourself, don't try and carry more than you can bear.

In practical terms, this may mean deferring university for a year, or taking a different job than the one you'd planned in order to be closer to friends and home. It may mean not sitting exams this year, or it may mean allowing yourself more money to spend on phone calls to friends and family. Getting on in the outside world is not always at all easy after a parent's death. In the first year after a bereavement, widows and widowers are advised not to make any drastic changes in their lives, such as changing job, moving house or getting married, but for young people this advice is often unrealistic.

One man of twenty-one heard, two weeks before his final exams at university, that his father had killed himself. An eighteen-year-old's father dropped dead the week she was due to leave home. A twenty-year-old girl learnt that her boyfriend had been killed in a car crash a month after they got engaged. It is scary enough being poised on the edge of adult life without having to cope with a parent's death at the same time. To cope with so many new situations you will sometimes find it necessary to delay grieving for a while. As long as you are only delaying, that is fine. It is thinking that grief can be avoided that leads to difficulties in the long term.

Essentially, facing a parent's death – any death – means facing the fact that you are out of control. You cannot know what is happening to you, nor how long it will go on for. You have to be patient and easy on yourself – and that is *all* you can do. This aspect of mourning a death is particularly difficult for young people, because it comes at a time in your life when you need to feel very much in control, to feel you are shaping your life and your future, making the right decisions about what subjects to study, what college to go to, what house to buy. It is hard to have confidence in your ability to make these kinds of decisions when you barely know what mood you will be in from one moment to the next, when you are depressed or irritable for no obvious reason. This stage in your life is when you take the control out of your parents' hands and into your own, when you take responsibility for yourself. Usually this process happens gradually, sometimes peacefully, sometimes with a great deal of yelling and fighting on the way. When a parent dies you find you suddenly have a lot more responsibility for yourself than you bargained for, at the same time as suddenly feeling far less in control of yourself and the world than before.

Don't underestimate how hard it is to adjust to a new world full of new people, new routines, new surroundings, new demands and expectations, especially at a time when you have no secure base to spring from. Living away from home for the first time, whether alone or in a shared house, can be hard to handle when you are bereaved. Time spent alone can be frightening. It is time for your mind to fill up with unwanted memories and painful images. It can also be hard to cope with other people whose problems seem to you so petty compared with the death of a parent and who seem to have all the confidence and complacency about life that you now lack. It can be upsetting not to be in your familiar surroundings with your possessions around you at a time when you crave some kind of stability and familiarity in your life.

When I arrived at university, I wondered how on earth I was going to cope with this brave new world when I was standing on what felt like quicksand. It was all right for them, I thought, they had firm foundations beneath them. But my world, in contrast, was infirm, shaky, unreliable. If the 'aliveness' of my parents could not be relied upon, what on earth could? How could I deal with all these new demands when it took all the energy I had just to believe that my mother and brothers and sisters were still, somewhere, alive and well. Some days the effort of believing that was tiring enough to leave nothing over for metaphysical poets and reformation drama. It certainly did not leave much over for making new friends, which I discovered also requires a firm base of self-confidence and *joie de vivre*. I felt wary of the world around me, and envied the other students their easy confidence and casual trust in the world.

For some people, however, making changes can be a help at a difficult time. For instance, it may be easier for you to have some distance and space between you and your family, particularly if you have had to take on a lot of responsibility for other members of the family and have not had room to feel your own grief and loss. You may also find that through work or college you meet people who have also been through the death of a parent, and who can help you cope with what you are going through. You may find, as Hillaire Belloc put it, that 'the laughter and the love of friends' is very comforting, and you may welcome a degree of normality in your life, the opportunity to 'forget' from time to time.

Whatever you decide to do, handle yourself with kid gloves through these changes, take smaller steps rather than bigger ones if possible. Try not to cut yourself off entirely from the old familiar places and people. Allow yourself access to them if it helps you deal with new and unfamiliar things in your life. Tell people around you who need to know what has happened; then at least you need not pretend to be fine when you are not – you have enough to worry about without worrying about how well you're pretending not to be worrying!

Help yourself to carry the weight of these additional losses. Allow yourself to find ways of minimizing the pain of loss and alleviating the sorrow of goodbyes, departures and separations, which you will probably feel far more heavily than others of your age.

• Coping with difficult emotions

Saying to yourself, 'My parent didn't mean to die. I must not

185

be angry', is not going to help you very much. Of course your parent didn't mean to die, but nevertheless they did die and their death has created problems for you and the rest of your family. Accepting that you do feel angry, that you are not happy about all the upheaval in your life can be very difficult, but is perfectly appropriate. And sometimes it is anger at these injustices which gives you the energy to keep going. Denied anger can lead to depression, which is far more dangerous in the long run. Anger that never ends is not healthy, of course, but anger roused by the immediate difficulties you are now facing is a normal and helpful response. Of course you are angry: bereavement does not turn us into saints.

One useful technique for dealing with anger is an exercise called 'How dare you!'. On a piece of paper simply write down everything you can think of that is making you angry. Don't think too hard, just let the words come into your head and write them down. They need not even be thoughts associated explicitly with death. Anything is fine, so long as each sentence you write begins with the words, 'How dare you . . .'

'How dare you die! How dare you leave us! How dare you not make a will! How dare you make us have to move house! How dare you upset us all like this! How dare you upset me! How dare you make it difficult for me to revise for my exams! How dare you ruin my love life! How dare you shake my life upside down like this . . .'

Whatever comes to mind, put it down. You will almost certainly find that the seething anger you so fear turns instead into a righteous indignation which asserts your needs and rights at a time when events are conspiring to ignore them. You will probably also find that the anger you may have feared was so great it would engulf the world, is not in fact so terrifyingly vast. It will exhaust itself, simmer down and stop, if you can let it out into the open for a bit. Bottled up anger seems to get bigger and bigger, it grows to horrifying proportions in the darkness of the heart. Don't be frightened of your anger. Undoubtedly it is one of the most difficult and unacceptable emotions bereavement will throw at you, but try to accept it and trust that it is there for good reasons. Try to find non-destructive ways of expressing it. You will probably find in doing so that your anger is not purely anger, it has in it strands of other feelings, such as loneliness, regret, sadness, fear. These feelings also need to be accepted and felt. They too have a right to be.

My sister developed her own version of the 'How dare you' technique. She has a book in which she writes letters to her father whenever she feels the need; sometimes they are sad letters, sometimes angry letters, sometimes funny ones. It is a valuable way of remaining in communication with her father through times when she still very much needs to communicate, when there are things she finds she still needs to say to him.

J. William Worden in *Grief Counselling and Grief Therapy* explains another technique called 'The empty chair' which is sometimes used in counselling. A chair is positioned on the opposite side of the room and you say to the chair, as if your parent were actually sitting in it, all the things you have been longing to say to them, from 'I miss you' to 'Damn you, how could you do this to me?'

It can be very helpful to have an outlet for these thoughts and feelings. It gets them out of your system where they would otherwise fester. It also helps to say or write those things explicitly, to hear that they are not so unreasonable, that it is not so peculiar to be angry or full of self-pity or frightened. The important thing with all these techniques is to address the dead person directly. Dreams often allow you to do this, but awake you may feel a bit silly doing this at first. Nevertheless it is an effective way of relieving the tension of having thoughts and feelings with no home to go to, as well as helping you to identify exactly what it is that you are thinking and feeling.

It is important not to think you must be a saint and it is important not to turn the dead person into a saint either. Telling them how much they have hurt you, how difficult they have made things for you, how hard you are finding life without them, how selfish it was of them to die, helps keep you both human. In the long run it is easier to mourn for a human being than for a saint. It is also easier to *live* with a human being than a saint, and ultimately, when you have mourned your dead, it is vital to find ways of living with them.

In one of Saul Bellow's novels, a character called Wilhelm who is separated from his wife, out of work, out of money, miserable about his mother's death, and not getting on well with his father, says to himself:

> Everyone was like the faces on a playing card,
> upside down either way.

(from *Seize the Day*)

This is how it is when someone dies: nothing is right, nothing is how it should be, everything is all twisted and confused and turned upside down whichever way you look at it. A death changes everything. Nothing is as it was. Everything is strange and unfamiliar, particularly those most familiar things like the chair where your father always sat and which now stands in the corner of the room embarrassing everyone with its emptiness. Like the dress which hangs unworn in the cupboard. Like the faces of your brothers and sisters, pale and slightly distorted with sorrow. No one can quite bear to look anyone else straight in the eye. Your remaining parent still appears the same, but is profoundly altered, may even seem to you to *smell* different. Things that had no significance before suddenly are full of significance – a hat, a pipe, a football. And things that were once significant are now grey with insignificance, totally meaningless – mealtimes, exams, the part-time job going at the newsagent. Nothing is unaltered by death. Accepting that change will happen and that after a parent's death certain changes will be, for you, extremely painful is vital. It can make it easier to recognize and cope with not only the changes but the difficult feelings they may rouse in you.

8

Old grief in new guises

*'There is no present
and no future; only
the past happening
over and over again.'*
(Eugene O'Neill)

One of the most difficult aspects of learning to live with a parent's death is that the process often continues in painful stages for many years, some would even say for the rest of your life. Accepting just how long the legacy of loss continues to make itself felt is one of the hardest aspects of a bereavement. Long, long after the actual event of a parent's death, the ripples and reverberations are still affecting your life. Sometimes you can feel as if there is no escape from the past, it just keeps coming back to haunt you, but sometimes it can return in ways that are hard to recognize and easy to ignore. Often it will seem ludicrous to connect the way you are feeling and behaving with your parent's death, but far below the surface of conscious thought the impact of such a loss *will* still be affecting your life. It will take a long time to learn to live with this hole in the centre of your world, particularly when the

191

hole reappears in so many different guises. recognize old grief when it appears in new guises can be an immense help.

Like most people, I have experienced the recurrence of old grief in new guises many times since the deaths of my father and step-father. And somehow, it always manages to take me by surprise. Seemingly unconnected events have the power to bring all the old pain and anguish flooding back, even years later. Perhaps the most surprising and shocking time this happened to me was when I was twenty-seven. My boyfriend (who would later become my husband) had to go abroad unexpectedly on business for a few weeks and we were parted for the first time in our relationship. I was totally unprepared for the passionate and agonizing sense of loss that would be ushered in by his departure. Left alone in the English countryside, where the spring blossomed into summer, I grieved. The sudden departure and abrupt absence of someone I loved very deeply revived all the most painful feelings of loss that I had gone through after my father died *ten years previously*. All the fear of death, of irreversible loss, of my own uselessness in the face of death, and all my fear of the pain of loss reared its head – as ugly and terrifying as ever. Until then I had begun to think I had covered over the wounds of my father's death with fresh skin – the spot was still inclined to be a little tender but the wound was healed. How massively I had underestimated the depth of those wounds! Following my boyfriend's departure I realized that they still reached into every corner of my heart and mind.

Those weeks were unabated mental and emotional agony. Finding myself suddenly bereft of a person I had grown to need and want to be near, I was plunged into despair, felt lost, inadequate, invisible, impotent. I was angry with my partner for going away, for leaving me a prey to all these old agonies, for subjecting me to this assault from my past. It was the same anger I felt after my father died, anger at the injustice, the impotence, the fear, the lack of care. I felt battered, broken, abused all over again by feelings of loss.

Repeatedly I told myself to be patient, that it was only a few weeks and that he would soon be back. But my mind was not my own; it performed acrobatics of its own accord, and when I tried to be calm and rational about my feelings, my mind would somersault and shriek with unkind laughter: 'How can you be so stupid? Why should he come back? Your father didn't. Neither did your step-father – and he only went for the weekend. Who are you kidding? He's probably dead already.' 'No, no, no, no,' I'd tell myself, 'he's fine, he's coming back.' At which my mind would do a crafty back flip to say, 'There are more ways of losing someone than death, you know. What if, at this very moment perhaps, he decides he doesn't love you any more?' 'Don't be stupid' I'd shout back, 'of course he still loves me. This is ridiculous!' 'But what if . . .' said my mind with a little cartwheel, 'and who's to say that maybe you don't love him either? Punish him for leaving you. Leave him! Let him have a taste of his own medicine! See how he likes it.'

If my mind was spritely and agile, emotionally and physically I felt as if I had undergone major surgery. Parts of me had been savagely removed and I was less than whole. I had no energy or concentration for anything, roamed listlessly from room to room, searching without even quite realizing what I was searching for. I tried to watch TV, stared gloomily at the flowers outside in the burgeoning summer, could not sleep, could not even eat.

Yet so much of all this was familiar. All these feelings and

193

thoughts were there when my father died: the disbelief that makes you wander through the house in a vague hope that you will find them; the numbing tiredness that sends you to bed with limbs like lead and prods you awake with a throbbing headache; the doubts and recriminations that make you think it is your fault that this dreadful thing has happened, that you somehow caused it and deserve it, that maybe if you had been nicer, quieter, prettier, cleverer, whatever, it wouldn't have happened; the fear that you will never be better, never ever be able to smile or laugh again, that happiness for you is a thing of the past; the sensation of being damaged, broken in some way deep inside; the rage, that makes you hate the person for causing you this anguish, for leaving you in this way, for failing to care for you as they should, for changing the rules of the game; the surge of emotions, so difficult to face that you either cannot eat with sickness, or eat too much to stifle the feelings that otherwise will stifle you.

My boyfriend's absence, the sudden, abrupt and total dislocation from his physical presence seemed somewhere in my mind like death. Each time the phone rang I sprang to pick up the receiver thinking 'It may be him', and sometimes it *was* him. But even then there was pain: the violent collision between the fantasy that he was dead and the proof of his aliveness made me feel I was going mad; hearing his voice I would be confused into silence, could only think: 'But how can it be him? So he *is* alive?', because quietly working away in the back of my mind through all the hours and minutes of our separation was the certain knowledge that he was dead and now my brain was totally befuddled! My rational brain and my profound irrational fantasies tussled over the evidence. After my father died I would leap to answer the phone when it rang, unable to stop the voice in my head saying 'It might be Dad calling', remembering only afterwards that Dad had been buried a fortnight before. And now there was this other much-loved much-mourned voice on the other end of the line asking how I was, what I'd been doing, and I had no reply other than the unutterable truth: 'Killing you in my imagination and reliving the past.'

Utterly confused by my boyfriend's absence, without any way of understanding it other than as a kind of death, I found myself terrified of the possibility that he really might die. I tormented myself with the thought and felt, once again, entirely alone with these terrible fears. In the same way as I had once felt unable to explain or share or receive adequate sympathy for the father I had lost, I now found myself convinced that no one else could possibly understand how vital this absent but living man was to me. How could they know that I could not now live without him? How could they appreciate how terrified I was that he would not return? And if my worst fears were realized, how could they begin to understand that I had lost what was most precious to me in the whole world? No one possibly could. I was lost once more, alone, lonely beyond belief.

And there I was, killing him again!

It was as if, ten years on, the death of my father still prevented me from making the imaginative leap from death to temporary separation. In my mind the two were one and the same. There was no difference. Away meant dead, and even though I knew this was not so, equally with another part of my mind, I knew it was so. Unlike people who have never experienced a bereavement, I could not pretend that death does not happen. I knew, for a fact – and a fact bedded in my own sorrow – that it did, that people you loved sometimes did die, that sometimes you'd speak to a person on the phone at night and in the morning that person was dead. However much I told myself – sternly, fiercely, angrily, even kindly – that my boyfriend in all probability would not die, that because it had happened before did not mean it would happen again, still it was the most fantastic struggle to silence my chattering brain and override the tide of panic.

As I struggled with my fears I realized not only the extent to which I still found separation difficult and distressing, but also that I had not until then fully committed myself to anyone since my father's death (although I had tried several times). Some quality of loving had receded deep inside at that time and not come to the surface again until now. And now that it had, the association between that quality of love for someone and the possibility of losing them was incredibly painful. At some level I was again the eighteen year old, confused, bewildered and betrayed by the sudden disappearance of my father from the physical and emotional stage of my life.

I was suffering from a bad case of 'old grief in new guises'.

• Old wine in new bottles

People are not unlike wine bottles, full of a heady mixture of emotions and thoughts provoked by all the business of the day, the week, the month, from a loving word, a good film, a sad item on the radio or an argument with a friend. A major event in your life, such as moving house or getting married, will fill you to overflowing with emotion. But when the bottle is so full it can be hard to find space for feelings stirred by the ordinary everyday occurences. After the traumatic event of a parent's death when you can find yourself flooded with feelings you simply don't have room for, you may well need to put some of the overflow into new bottles. The problem is that these new bottles are easy to mislabel. Instead of 'Bereavement' or 'Grief' or 'Mum's death', you may have stuck on a label saying, 'Wrong job', 'Rotten teacher', 'Drugs', 'Boyfriend trouble' or 'Anorexia'. One of the hardest and most prolonged tasks of grieving is to recognize when a bottle has been wrongly labelled and that what you are tasting is the same old wine as before, the same old grief in a new guise.

There are basically two ways in which you may encounter old wine in new and wrongly labelled bottles.

First, when events in your life (which perhaps involve some kind of loss) reactivate painful emotions connected with your parent's death and then become hard to handle because they are now emotionally charged beyond their true significance.

Secondly, when feelings of grief are not allowed to be felt in direct relation to your parent's death or to the relationship you had with them while they were alive, and therefore have to find new ways of coming out. Old grief may come up in new guises in the first months of a bereavement, but equally it may emerge years, even decades, later.

As a child, Pippa had craved the attention of her mother, who tended instead to ignore her and spoil her pretty younger sister. When her mother died, when Pippa was sixteen, Pippa's hopes of ever getting that attention died too and subconsciously she accepted that from then on she was destined to be the least favoured one in any group. Some time after her mother's death, Pippa found herself working for a difficult, bullying woman who persistently praised her counterpart in the office and omitted to praise her. Pippa found herself re-experiencing all the painful feelings of her childhood, feeling once again the helplessness of the child ignored by her mother. It took a while to make this connection between her mother's neglect and her employer's neglect, and even afterwards it was still very hard for her to stand up against her employer's unfair and unprofessional behaviour. It was difficult to remember that she was no longer the powerless child, but an adult able to act like an adult, with the power of words and actions on her side.

When there is a large parent-shaped gap in your life, a teacher or tutor or boss can start to fill that space, sometimes in a positive way, as a guide or mentor, but sometimes negatively, as Pippa discovered.

I was lucky in my first job to have an exceptionally nice employer. It was my first experience of living in London and my first experience of living on my own, and I think I did more grieving that year than in the previous three for the simple reason that for the first time there was time and space for myself. The deaths of my father and my step-father were still raw inside me, but I was frightened by them, frightened that I would never 'get over it', never be 'normal' again. I wanted more than anything to be like all the other young people that I saw on the Underground, in the office, wandering round the shops in Covent Garden at lunchtimes: good-looking, happy, carefree. Instead I was me pretending. I was me – worried, anxious, insecure, fearful – acting out this idea of how young people ought to be. The effort of the pretence was exhausting and, as often happens when people are under stress and working against rather than with themselves, I began to be plagued with small ailments, colds, coughs, bouts of flu, days of feeling tearful and low. I worried about how much time I was taking off work, but what could I do? I always seemed to be going down with some illness or other. One day I met my boss in the corridor and he asked how I was feeling. On an impulse I decided to be honest rather than brave. I admitted that I was pretty miserable and finding it hard to get going again after two bereavements. To my surprise a look of relief came over his face. 'Oh, I wish you'd told me before,' he said, kindly, 'I didn't know what was going on, I thought maybe you were hating the job or something. I could have been more help to you if I'd known what the matter was.'

Not all bosses are this nice, nor all teachers: all too often problems at work or school are overlooked or misunderstood through the insensitivity of employers and teachers. But sometimes school or work is a 'new bottle' for the 'old wine' of your grief. It may be worth stopping to ask yourself if they or the situation remind you of how things were at home before your parent died. A bullying, unjust, exacting boss can remind you of a father or mother who also may have bullied you or treated you unfairly, in turn making you inappropriately tolerant or intolerant of the situation. Similarly a critical teacher may remind you of a critical parent. 'She's just like my bloody mother,' you might have said when your parent was still alive and fought against it. Now, with all the complicated reactions of grief, you might at some level believe you have to take this criticism, perhaps because it somehow makes you feel close to your dead parent, or perhaps because you feel it is just punishment for your negative feelings towards your parent when he or she was alive.

In *A Secure Base*, John Bowlby describes the case of a man

199

of twenty-seven who became suicidally depressed after splitting up with his girlfriend. He also started to suffer from a range of physical sensations, including a feeling of choking. With the help of therapy, and a sensitive and alert analyst, he was able to unearth a long-buried memory of witnessing his mother's attempted suicide when he was a small boy. Certain similarities in the way he broke up with his girlfriend had triggered a memory of this traumatic event.

If losing a lover can stir painful feelings and memories after twenty-five years, it is not so strange to be reminded of the death of a parent only two or three years back when you split up with a partner, especially if there are difficult thoughts and feelings that you have until now avoided.

Not that long after Sian's father died, she also had to cope with splitting up with her boyfriend. They had been together for almost ten years, since they were teenagers, and although the relationship had its problems, she always thought they would stay together. One day, however, she came home to find her boyfriend had moved out. These two losses so close to each other were terrible for her. She felt as if her whole life was crumbling around her. She was furious with her boyfriend for leaving her when she needed him, but at the same time she still believed he would come back to her. Sian justified her hopes that her boyfriend would return by reasoning that her father's death had perhaps triggered painful memories for him because his own father had died when he was a child. It was his bereavement that he was running away from, she reasoned, not their relationship. Whatever his reasons for leaving, the boyfriend never did come back and he left Sian with two losses to come to terms with, which she did only with great difficulty. All her negative, hostile feelings she attributed to her boyfriend, while all her positive, sad feelings she directed towards her father. She could believe that her father was dead, but she could not believe that her boyfriend had left her. The truth of the matter was that she needed to believe, and to come to terms with, both these facts.

Sian found, and this is not uncommon, that when there are unresolved and complicated feelings for the person who has died, it is possible to face some of those feelings about that person and the death, but others get stashed away until another target can be found for them. In Sian's case, many of the feelings of rage and hostility and contempt that she felt towards her boyfriend were feelings she had long harboured towards her father, but which she could not admit to feeling.

In Jane Austen's novel *Northanger Abbey*, seventeen year old Catherine Morland learns that the mother of her friend, Eleanor Tilney, had died some years before.

> 'Her death must have been a great affliction!'
> 'A great and increasing one,' replied the other, in a low voice. 'I was only thirteen when it happened; and though I felt my loss perhaps as strongly as one so young could feel it, I did not, I could not then know what a loss it was.'

Eleanor shows an insight in her words about the continuing effects of a parent's death that most of us unfortunately lack; she displays an honest, if painful, acceptance of how long the repercussions of grief are felt. Recognizing the continuing influence of the past in the patterns of the present can make it easier to separate past from present. Realizing how new problems in your life may be related to old ones is the first vital step towards making sense of things, the first step towards labelling your wine bottles properly.

Nevertheless it *is* shocking how an event years after your parent died can catapult you right back into the fears and anxieties of the time immediately surrounding the death.

It helps a little to understand that these may be 'old' feelings, that your reactions may be more appropriate to then than now, (although the experience is not any the less intense or harrowing or real for that little bit of calm rationality that can say, 'This is old business.') It can also help to be prepared for the resurrection of these old painful feelings in certain new situations, because if you can anticipate them it allows you to prepare a little for them, to find ways of cushioning the blow of those thoughts and feelings, and to protect yourself from their impact. Most importantly, recognizing and anticipating the real genesis of these emotions makes them easier to live with, and in turn makes it easier not to punish yourself for feeling miserable, angry, resentful, confused . . . You can, at the very least, not add guilt and shame to an already seething pot of feelings.

The extraordinary force and power and resilience of these irrational frightening thoughts is quite something, and the difficulties that exist in overcoming them are very real, even when you know them to be irrational and unrealistic. Even when you can argue with yourself, can understand the source of these thoughts and feelings, they still hold you in their grip.

• Repeating patterns

Psychologists and psychoanalysts have long recognized the way in which people repeat patterns in their lives until they can look at what is going on and understand fully why these things are happening. As George Santayana put it: 'Those who cannot remember the past are condemned to repeat it.'

The particular pattern of repetition will be different for everyone: for some people it is the boss they simply cannot get on with no matter how often they change jobs, no matter how hard they work; for others it is a specific habit like always getting drunk before an important event, habitually getting caught speeding, or continually falling out with friends. But until people recognize the underlying cause of these events, they will unconsciously re-create situations in which they are forced to go through the same emotions.

It is not unlike the way a musician practises a difficult phrase of music. It won't be the same sequence of notes in a piece of music that creates problems for every musician, but the process of getting those notes right is the same: unless the musician stops and sorts out why she or he can't play that particular bit, works out whether it is the fingering, the timing or the articulation that is causing the problem, she or he will continue to stumble and falter at that same point. Stopping and practising once may not be enough to solve the problem immediately; maybe it will be necessary to go over a passage or phrase many times before it can be managed without faltering. Life is like this too.

It took one man fifteen years to work out the 'passage' that he repeatedly stumbled at but eventually, when his personal life had got into serious disarray, he was forced to stop and look at what was happening. Only then did he really understand for the first time how the element of pain involved in loving someone had become intolerable after his mother died when he was seventeen, and how in a desperate and futile attempt to protect himself from pain he had shut out love by ending the relationship he was in at the time of her death. When a few years later his father remarried and he 'lost' him in some sense, he did it again, slammed down the emotional hatch, ended a relationship. Over the next ten years all his relationships had got stuck at the first sign of difficulties: when the going got tough, when love involved pain, he found it intolerable and refused to go on. It gave him a sense of power at a time when he felt powerless and out of control of his life.

Angela 'practised' her fears too, but was able to work out the problem before things got out of hand. She started going out with her boyfriend a year after her father died. He was kind and affectionate and helped her recover her confidence in herself and in life – up to a certain point. That point was his passion for rock-climbing. Every other weekend or so he went off, leaving Angela convinced it was the last time she would see him. She lived his death in her imagination every second that he was away. When he came back, safe and sound, she was exhausted with worry and in a state of silent rage that he had inflicted so much pain on her so unnecessarily. She hated herself for not 'coping' and blamed herself for her suffering as much as she blamed him. It took a long time but eventually she began to see that in the circumstances it was not surprising she was so frightened by his rock-climbing, and that what *was* wrong was putting herself through such an ordeal on a regular basis. In the context of her father's recent death, she could not be expected to cope equably with these separations. Her boyfriend would not or could not understand how distressing and destructive his risk-taking was and in the end he and Angela decided to go their separate ways.

Her fear and distress was the old wine of her grief in the new bottle of his rock-climbing. Recognizing that her feelings were related to an earlier event made it easier for Angela to understand and accept her fear and find ways of looking after herself instead of needlessly hurting herself further. She too turned her back on a relationship but in her case it was for positive reasons.

The Secret Garden, a classic children's book by Frances Hodgson Burnett, is about two bereaved children whose lives have 'got stuck'. Colin is an invalid and terrified he is going to die. He is unable to tolerate any difficulties or obstructions and when they do occur is thrown into a hysterical frenzy. He is a child assaulted by the past, his tantrums express the fear-filled panic of a child whose mother has died and whose life has fallen apart. He says at one point 'I wish I had died too.' But in the course of the story, he learns that there is a way through these moments of fear, that old painful feelings must be looked at and that obstacles in life are also challenges that can be turned to his own advantage. Through his friendship with Mary, he begins to live with enthusiasm for the present and hope for the future. The locked-up secret garden, which the children discover and gradually bring to life, is a powerful image for the 'stuck' state that all bereaved people must confront at some time or other. Unless the symbolic tangle of thorny bushes in the secret garden, or the problematic sequence of notes in a piece of music, are looked at and gone over and worked out, the legacy of bereavement can continue to trap you for years and years, sometimes in dangerous and life-threatening ways.

Neil was in his forties when he decided to train as a social worker. His marriage had recently collapsed and he wanted to build a new life for himself. As part of his training he was required to do a project and he chose the impact of bereavement as his subject. However, as his research progressed he became more and more depressed and finally sought his supervisor's help. Neil arrived in the supervisor's office in desperation and within a few minutes he was sobbing uncontrollably. When he had calmed down a little he and his supervisor began to talk; gentle questioning soon revealed that his mother had died when Neil was in his early twenties, but he had been too frightened to grieve for her and had simply buried all his feelings about her death. He had made no conscious connection between his own buried grief and the decision to study bereavement for his coursework, and the force of his own twenty-year-old loss emerging now it had the chance was deeply shocking to him, as well as necessary.

For Evelyn, on the other hand, it was the opportunity for emotional stability rather than collapse of it that acted as a catalyst for her long-buried grief. Her mother had died when Evelyn was twelve. When she was in her early thirties her boyfriend with whom she'd been living for many years decided it was high time they made a firm commitment to one another and got married. Although Evelyn had no previous intention of leaving her boyfriend, his proposal of marriage set in chain an entirely unexpected series of emotions in her which resulted in her ending the relationship altogether. Through counselling she began to realize how her panic about marriage was more connected with fear of death and unfinished grieving than her choice of life-partner. As a child she had seemed fairly unaffected by her mother's death and continued to be a cheerful, optimistic girl. As an adult she was successful in her career, popular with her friends and happy with her partner. The sudden prospect of marriage had brought with it all kinds of issues about having a home and a family of her own, being loved and cherished, being committed to one person for the rest of her life, issues that in turn reactivated long-buried fears. As a little girl left alone with her grieving father, she had imagined herself somehow to blame for her mother's death and therefore undeserving of her father's love. She saw herself as destructive and unlovable. To compensate she had forced herself always to be extra-nice, extra-cheerful, extra-undemanding. How could Evelyn now accept her partner's offer of love-for-life when she held inside her this frightening knowledge of her power to destroy love? How could she commit herself to one person and run the risk of losing him too? Her partner's proposal had opened the door for all the confused but still powerful thoughts and feelings from her childhood, leaving her bewildered and scared and near to collapse.

It can be tempting — and sometimes necessary – to try to avoid the perplexing symptons of grief and people often do: they change job a lot; they change partner a lot; they go abroad; they move house every six months. Any substantial degree of commitment, be it to a place, a job, or a person, rouses the painful possibility of loss. Having something makes you think how it would be not to have it. If in the past you decided that loss was unbearably painful and therefore all future pain should be avoided by never risking loss, to a certain extent you are protecting yourself from difficult emotions, but inevitably you lose out, because by avoiding the consequences of losing anything, you avoid also the consequences of ever really having anything. History and literature and psychology books are full of accounts of people whose lives have remained empty of love, fulfilment and happiness because they could not bear the possibility of their opposites: loss, loneliness, sadness. The irony is that they ended up with those feelings anyway without having had the pleasure of the others.

Unlike homework or games lessons or office parties, grief is not something that can be avoided. There is no question of avoiding grief. People sometimes imagine they can. They shut down inside, freeze up, simply refuse to let themselves feel the pain of their loss, the anger, sadness, confusion, guilt. They button themselves up and stiffen their upper lip and say, 'Well, can't sit around here moping', or 'Dad would hate me to fail my exams', or 'It's not so bad, other people have far worse things happen to them', or 'No time to think about my problems, I've got to make sure the rest of the family is all right now that Mum is dead'.

All these thoughts may be appropriate at some point, but perhaps not right now. Using thoughts like these to keep difficult emotions under control is a short-term strategy for survival, not a long-term route to recovery. Time tends to reveal that on the contrary people who have gained control in this way have not even begun to 'get over it', but succeeded only in delaying the moment when they must grieve. The moment when the stored-up grief wells up and bursts out is more, not less, painful for the intervening years, as Evelyn, Neil and countless others, myself included, have discovered.

It is as if you had been to a party at which everybody was in jeans and, not wanting to stick out, you had to wear jeans too. The problem was that your jeans no longer fitted and you had to lie on the floor to haul them on and hold your breath to do up the zip. All evening you could hardly move, but at least you were there at the party, looking pretty much like everyone else. From time to time you wondered to yourself if other people could tell that your jeans were way too tight, but on the whole you just felt relieved that you'd managed not to draw attention to yourself by being the odd one out. At the end of the evening you got home, held your breath to undo the zip, struggled with the button and at last exhaled: the zip flew apart and your stomach bulged out through the gap. There were red marks on your hips where the seams had pressed and even some little bruises where the studs had pushed into your flesh. For the first time you realized how incredibly uncomfortable you'd been all evening.

Imagine then deciding to wear those too-tight jeans not for an evening but all the time, every second of every minute of every day, not even allowing yourself to take them off at night. Imagine what a mangled crushed mess you would be inside after years in that ungiving casement of cloth. You might find yourself quite helpless, the muscles and bones so squashed and stiff that you could no longer walk without the denim mould. This may sound far-fetched but it happens.

If grief is squashed up into some tiny place inside you while you wrap yourself in an armour of unfeeling, it is likely that at some time in the future when you find yourself under pressure or strain, maybe from work, maybe through problems in a relationship, maybe because of another death, maybe even through a happy but still stressful event like having a baby or moving house, the armour will no longer be enough to protect you. The grief will not have disappeared, not even after a decade or more, it will just have grown older and stiffer, more brittle and more unyielding. Less easy to cope with perhaps, but just as real.

William Styron, who wrote the book and screen play for the film *Sophie's Choice*, describes in his recent book *Darkness Visible* how giving up drink after years of using it as a protection against the inner world of dark and troubling emotions and thoughts catapulted him into a nervous breakdown. He was then in his sixties, but in the months following the breakdown, he began to attribute a life-time of alcohol abuse and recurrent depressions – which although he denied them, had gathered like storm-clouds – to his mother's death when he was a teenager. He writes of 'an insufferable burden, of which rage and guilt, and not only dammed-up sorrow, are a part'. These, he says, were 'the potential seeds of self-destruction'. He goes on:

... disorder and early sorrow – the death or disappearance of a parent, especially a mother, before or during puperty – appears repeatedly in the literature on depression as a trauma sometimes likely to create nearly irreparable emotional havoc.

It is important to realize that grief may emerge in new guises in the first months of a bereavement, but equally it may come up years, even decades, after a parent's death. It is this old grief that plays such havoc in people's lives when it appears later on in new and strange ways, in the places and at the times they least expect it to. The pressures on young people make it particularly hard to grieve at the time and therefore leave you particularly vulnerable to delayed or denied grief. It is therefore young people especially who need to understand the peculiar workings of old grief.

9   Hurting yourself to avoid the pain

'Only people who avoid love can avoid grief. The point is to learn from it and remain vulnerable to love.'

Peopl are extraordinarily adept and ingenious in their attempts to shut out painful feelings, but then painful feelings are just as adept and ingenious at making themselves felt. Often the person who gets harmed, unwittingly, by this struggle is you.

It is extremely hard to feel loving and kindly towards yourself when a parent has died and when the world around you seems to be so cruel and uncaring. Somehow it can seem easier just to join in. Perhaps there is even a kind of comfort to be had from being the one to inflict the pain, rather than having it inflicted at least you have a sense of control instead of the dreadful feeling of impotence that comes with a parent's death.

The desire and need to feel in control and thereby regain at least some sense of power over your life is always very keen after a bereavement, but it is particularly so in your teens and twenties when the issues of power and control are all-important.

Perhaps you are living away from home for the first time, setting your own rules about what time you get in, who you see, what you eat. With increased power over your life comes also an increased awareness of vulnerability and responsibility; the gain of control also brings with it a loss of safety: out in the world now you may feel exhilarated by the freedom but simultaneously a little apprehensive about it. If, on the other hand, you are still living at home, the restriction of your parents' rule may be getting more and more irritating as each week passes. You feel old enough to be allowed to make your own choices about what time to go to bed, whether or not to go to school, how often to see your friends, how much time you need for homework, but maybe – often, in fact – parents will disagree. Wanting control of your life yet feeling it is constantly withheld is a familiar and frustrating experience. Depending on your personality and particular circumstances, this sense of powerlessness can be anything from mildly annoying to very uncomfortable or even totally intolerable.

All things at this stage are double-edged and ambiguous, and that involves the shift from 'still at home' to 'in charge of your life'. It is not an instant or straightforward transition at the best of times; it involves uncertainty, reversals, abrupt breaks – and time. It is as much like a smooth ride as a rollercoaster in a force-ten gale – and that is *without* the added complication of bereavement.

With all these issues of control and lack of it, power and powerlessness, it is not surprising that when a parent dies, the need for some control of your life becomes even greater and makes it all the more terrifying to be so out of control, to have thoughts and feelings taking over at the most inconvenient and unexpected times. As one woman put it six months after her mother's death: 'The big pressures in my life aren't the problem, I can cope with those. It's when I'm washing up or just sitting quietly after supper that it really hurts.'

However much you crave control of these awful moments of surging pain and sorrow, it is very important to accept that control is not going to help matters in the long term if it has been gained by suppressing feelings that need to be expressed. There is a price to be paid for this kind of control: often you succeed in 'conquering' grief only by finding other, indirect ways of hurting yourself. Recognizing that you may be trying to control the uncontrollable is a big step towards helping yourself after a parent's death. And recognizing the ways in which you may be trying to get that control is of course vital.

• Hurting yourself with drugs

Judith was seventeen when her father died; she spent the next six months drinking heavily and taking drugs. She did not mind feeling out of control as long as she was the one to decide when and how it happened. What she could not tolerate was the involuntary 'out-of-control' caused by her father's death and her reaction to it. It seemed as if she had a drug problem; what she really had was a grief problem.

Jamie, aged fifteen, used drugs in a different way but for the same ultimate purpose: to feel in charge of a situation that was painfully out of his control. Jamie's father had died several years previously and he had suffered from terrible nightmares for some time afterwards. Although he had brothers and sisters, Jamie was the youngest and his mother's favourite, and after his father's death they became closer still. The problems began when his mother decided to remarry.

About the time that her future husband moved in, Jamie began to get involved with drugs and he was soon dealing, enjoying the money, status and power this brought. His mother, immersed in her new relationship and busy planning her wedding, noticed neither that her son was rather flush for a schoolboy, nor how many friends he suddenly seemed to have these days. She saw no cause to worry: he wasn't doing particularly well at school, but maybe that was his age and he would grow out of it. The week of the wedding Jamie was arrested for dealing and possession.

Later, in court, the probation officer linked his father's death and his mother's remarriage as prime causes, a connection neither Jamie nor his mother had made themselves until then, but which in retrospect began to make sense. Six years after his father's death her marriage still had the power to bring up old painful feelings of helplessness, but because they were so close, Jamie did not feel able to take out his feelings of rejection, insignificance and anxiety on his mother. Instead he turned his attention away from his family to the world of his friends for the approval and affirmation he needed and seemed about to lose.

Jamie didn't intend to get so involved with drugs, but they sucked him in, gave him the impression of taking possession of them as they, in reality, took possession of him. At first it seemed the perfect solution to his problems: a way of protesting at his diminished importance in his mother's life when for so long he had been all-important to her. Dealing was a way of overcoming the panicky sensation of being insignificant, invisible, pushed out. Suddenly people wanted to see him, treated him as if he mattered, as if he were important. He was suddenly somebody. He was powerful, no longer the helpless fifteen year old who had lost his father and was now about to lose his mother, but someone with authority, power, money, status. He was in control. But looked at another way, Jamie was not at all in control. Long before the police caught up with him, he was a prisoner of his desire for control, enslaved by his need to have money and status. And behind that desire and need was the same intense fear of being helpless and out of control that Judith experienced. It was a vicious circle which in some ways he had created for himself, a classic example of old wine in new bottles.

• Hurting yourself with sex

Some people try to gain control of their pain not through drugs or alcohol but through sex. Often they too end up hurting themselves.

Sex can be a way of feeling close to someone. The physical proximity of another person's body can be extremely comforting. The feeling of a pair of arms encircling you, the warmth of another person's flesh and the smell of another's skin can shut out the feeling that the world is a cold, hostile place. The physical presence of another person can make you feel more substantial and less fragile in a world that has become unreliable, uncertain, dangerous even.

Physical affection is profoundly necessary. Few better ways exist to ease the ache of loneliness. Having someone there who wants you, desires you and compliments you can be very

215

important when you are feeling abandoned, and – as people often do after a bereavement – somehow contaminated and to blame. Physical affection can stop the unpleasant sensation of having some disease that other people are afraid of catching if they get too close: the disease of unhappiness, the disease of death. When people seem to be looking at you with an expression in their eyes that says, 'I'm very sorry for you, but don't come too near,' it is incredibly sustaining to be made to feel physically O.K., to find that people do want to get near to you after all.

The physical presence of another person is not only comforting, it is also distracting. Another person's body against yours, another person's hands on your flesh, desire: all these distract you from the muddle in your head, the troubling chaos of emotions. Sex can even counteract the numbness that follows the death of a parent. Physical contact can make you feel alive again which can be very reassuring if you find the feeling of numbness alarming.

The problems start when physical affection and sex get confused and sex becomes the *only* way in which you can feel, the only thing that reawakens sensation, so you begin to crave it like a drug. It becomes a fix you are dependent on.

Alison was like that. After her mother's death, when she was nineteen, Alison became very promiscuous. She seemed to need sex: it made her feel normal, it made her feel real, it made her feel wanted. Most of all, it made her *feel*. The more men desired her, the more addicted she became to sex as a way of being. It gave her a sense of power at a time in her life when she felt powerless. It also gave her the sense that her own life had not stopped with her mother's death, but that she, Alison, was continuing to live. She knew that there was a destructive

216

element in her quest for physical sensation: not only did she rarely find lasting physical satisfaction or emotional solace in the men she went to bed with, she also seemed particularly drawn to people she did not know and whom it was actually quite risky to sleep with – perhaps because they injected drugs, or had a history of bisexuality or promiscuity. The greater the risk, the greater the attraction. It was as if in her apparent quest for life and feeling, Alison also was seeking a kind of destruction. She was at some level not healing herself but harming herself – and she knew it, but could not stop.

In some senses she was doing what was 'normal' for a nineteen year old: she was having boyfriends, having fun, getting laid, and laying. But it was all done in a kind of self-destructive frenzy. In the short periods when she was without a boyfriend, Alison would become beside herself with loneliness, self-hatred and feelings of failure. Before very long she would find another guy on whom to pin all her hopes of survival and rejuvenation, someone who would bring her to life by filling her with desire. This pattern of behaviour went on for some time: her love-life was the source of amazement and concern to those who cared about her. Alison herself was vaguely aware that there might be some connection between her behaviour and her mother's death but it seemed unlikely, as in other respects she had coped well with the death and the subsequent upheavals in her family. It was only after a prolonged bout of depression that Alison decided to have some counselling and at last began to recognize fully and understand the connection.

Alison's mother had always been rather strict and kept a close and often disapproving eye on Alison. She had vetted

Alison's friends and always imposed rules about how often her daughter went out in the week, how late she stayed out and where she was allowed to go. After her death, there were no rules any more, no guidelines, and in Alison's sex life there was both the frantic activity of the girl who did not quite know how to set her own rules, and also a kind of anger, a 'fuck you' attitude which seemed to be saying 'You're not here to look after me now, but how am I supposed to look after myself?'

Alison also began to understand how her boyfriends had fallen into two quite different categories: on the one hand there were the solid, reliable, steady types, and on the other there were the unpredictable, unreliable, dangerous types. The counsellor asked her, what did she want? A steady, reliable father or an exciting lover? In Alison's mind, there was no room for the reliable *and* exciting lover who might have satisfied her, because through her affairs she was playing out two different roles: the girl who deserved to be cared for and the girl who deserved to be punished.

Through the counselling sessions she discovered that she was carrying with her not only the positive memories she had of her mother, but also the more difficult memories of a woman who could be highly critical of her daughter, disapproving and censorious, often not talking to her for days on end. In particular her mother had frowned on Alison's boyfriends, frowned on any suggestion that her little girl was turning into a sexual woman. Alison began to see how she had often gone against her mother's wishes with regards to her choice of boyfriend, but that her mother's approval had nevertheless mattered greatly. Now that her mother was dead, who was to give her guidance? She had to carry around inside not only the judging critical voice of her mother, but also her

218

own voice busily rejecting her mother's opinion. Sex for Alison was a way of asserting her independence and punishing her mother for having died. Through sex she could say both 'I can do what I like. I can make up my own mind', and at the same time, 'I can't choose. I am helpless and hopeless without you. I need you.'

Sex can be life-affirming. It can also be a destructive, aggressive, hostile act. The existence of rape proves the possibility for aggression in sex. But both women and men can use sex as a weapon. Sometimes they use it against the other person and sometimes they use it against themselves.

Alex had a stream of girlfriends after his mother died, never staying much more than one night with any one of them. For him casual sex served a number of functions. It was a way of trying to get back to some warm safe place where he could for a while just forget himself, be relieved of himself, relieved of consciousness. It was a way of distracting himself: the chase was exhilarating and all-engrossing. Once he'd slept with the current object of his desire, however, all the excitement was gone and he'd have to start again with someone else. Sex made him feel powerful. It made him feel attractive, wanted, irresistible, important, successful. Filled with his own desire and his awareness of the girl's desire for him, he could shut out, briefly, all the troubling feelings of helplessness, powerlessness and insignificance that his mother's death had roused in him.

Sex also, and quite unconsciously, was a way of punishing his mother for dying. Alex was not easily angered. He had a reputation in his family for being patient and sweet-tempered. Nevertheless his mother's death left him feeling abandoned, bewildered and terribly hurt. He was angry with life for doing this to him, angry with his mother for dying and leaving him, for hurting him and for hurting his father and sister. By hurting other women, by showing how little he cared about their feelings, how insignificant they were to him, he was trying to show himself that he could be unaffected by his mother's death, that he could in fact hurt her, instead of being hurt. It was a long time before he understood the link between his mother's death and his promiscuity. Before that, like Alison, he went through a period of quite serious depression which prompted him to see a therapist. Over the course of several months, therapy helped him to see how he had been using sex to inure himself to the pain and confusion of grief, and at the same time using sex to get back at his mother for having died and left him.

You don't have to be promiscuous to hurt yourself with sex. Tasha started to go out with Martin very soon after her father died, when she was twenty-two. She had not intended or wanted to have a relationship with Martin, but he was very keen on her and because she was grateful to have someone there to comfort her and take her mind off her father's death, she found she had slipped into the relationship almost despite herself. She was desperate for someone to care for her, hold her, want her, soothe her, but while cuddles were comforting, sex was not. She felt intensely guilty to be having sex at all so soon after her father's death. It felt inappropriate to her. Furthermore she felt so vulnerable and fragile that the physical act of intercourse was almost unbearable. Being physically penetrated made her feel all the more vulnerable, but Tasha did not know how to explain all this to Martin. If she felt guilty about having sex, she also felt guilty about not wanting it. She was caught between two stools, on the one hand wanting to be normal and have fun and make love like other people of her age, and on the other hand needing to grieve for her father. She had quickly become dependent on Martin for his emotional support and was frightened that if she refused to have sex, he might get fed up with her and leave. Another loss, she felt, would be unendurable.

Tasha and Martin stayed together for two years, during which time the problems with their sex life did not improve. Tasha never really got over her initial deep ambivalence about whether or not she wanted to be having a sexual relationship with Martin. She convinced herself that she should want sex, but despite everything her head said, her body would not play. Throughout the time they were together, she had constant recurrences of cystitis and thrush. She also suffered from vaginismus (when the walls of the vagina go into spasm, making penetration very difficult and painful). All three of these conditions were related to stress and anxiety, but it was only after she had split up with Martin that she began to see the connection between the timing of the relationship – i.e. coinciding with her father's death – and the constant run of genito-urinary ailments. As she puts it now: 'At the time I was so determined to be the perfect girlfriend, to be fun and relaxed and good in bed, that I couldn't accept what my body was trying so hard to tell me. I made a kind of trade-off: if he hugged me and listened to me and was there for me, I would be there for him sexually. I simply didn't have the strength or courage to say no. I didn't like being boring and frigid. I wanted to be young and carefree. I was annoyed with myself for not being. Now I feel quite ashamed – of how little respect or love I showed myself. I'm angry with Martin too, if I'm honest, for not being more sensitive.'

221

Tasha was using sex to punish herself for not living up to her own expectations of what a girlfriend should be. It is also possible that if at first she didn't want to make love because she was grieving for her father, later she was punishing herself with sex for not living up to her expectations of what a perfect daughter and girlfriend should have been.

Thinking about the physical act of sex, it isn't hard to see why it seems to offer comfort. It fills you up, literally, or makes you feel contained. Usually a bereavement puts out the sexual lights for a while, and you may well feel anxious and despondent about the loss of sexual desire: after all, you say to yourself, shouldn't I be at my sexual peak? What if I get left behind? If you are worried, try not to forget that loss of desire is a *natural* response to the very traumatic experience of a parent's death.

Sometimes feelings of grief can be channelled into an increased sex drive, as in Alison and Alex's case, but if you are using sex to mask feelings that need to be dealt with, it can become a very destructive form of behaviour. Try to give yourself time to think about the emotions and fantasies you associate with sex: is it the momentary sensation of power that you like, or the obliteration of worries and cares? Is it the physical touch of someone's skin that you want? Or is sex a way of being aggressive that is somehow 'allowed'? There is nothing wrong with associating any of these feelings with sex, unless of course the sex is making you miserable and is not satisfying. If so, maybe you can isolate what you want from sex and find it in other ways. Maybe a better way of getting some caring touch is by having a massage. Maybe playing squash is a better way of expressing hostility and aggression.

• Hurting yourself with exercise

Even things that are generally regarded as good for you, such as exercise, can in fact be disguises for extremely unhealthy behaviour. Exercise can be a way not of getting fit but of avoiding painful feelings and keeping up the appearance of being in control of your life. But exercise can become an addiction as unhealthy as any other.

Dale's father died after a long and painful illness when Dale was twenty, and in the following years he used exercise to shut out the reality of his loss. He took up running shortly after his father's death ostensibly for health reasons, but for the next five years became as dependent on his daily run as a heroin addict on his fix. Every morning he had to run for at least two hours; whatever time he had gone to bed the night before, wherever he was in the world, whatever the weather, he ran. It gave him a feeling of calm, of transcendence. Dale also had a demanding job as a junior doctor which involved long hours and hard work. This, combined with his running schedule therefore left him no free time to reflect on how he felt about his father's death. He was afraid of quiet, contemplative, leisurely time, time alone, because time came accompanied by frightening possibilities for unwanted thoughts and feelings to emerge. So he ran and worked and kept a rigid control of those lurking unwanted complicated emotions that threatened to surface if he let up for a moment. But of course he suffered, not only from extreme fatigue, but also from leaving no room in his life for friends or relationships. Beneath the efficient, highly organized facade, lay great pain and loneliness that he simply could not bear to face.

• Hurting yourself with food

Another way of expressing emotions that seem otherwise

inexpressible is through food, whether by eating too much or not enough of it. You are hurting yourself with food if on a regular basis you use food in a way that has nothing to do with physical appetite or nutritional needs and everything to do with how you are feeling. Anorexia, bulimia and compulsive eating are the technical terms for the various forms of eating disorders. They are methods used primarily but not exclusively by young women. Certainly it was the method I used to try and gain control at a time when life felt out of my control.

My eating habits had been fairly chaotic since my father's death when I had used food to fill me up and give me comprehensible discomfort instead of the bewildering kind of discomfort caused by sorrow which I had no idea what to do with. I had eaten then to shut out feeling, or at least to provide an easy excuse for feelings I did not like – nausea and anxiety. After my step-father's death I went the other way and stopped eating, waged war on my appetite, determined to gain control of my own body which was so full of unwanted needs and troubling emotions.

At the same time as refusing to eat, I took responsibility for preparing meals for everyone else: somewhere in the back of my mind was the idea that if I could only keep people fed, I might somehow keep them alive, make them better; I might be able to fill the emptiness inside them, both literally with food and symbolically with my care and love. But at the same time as I imagined myself responsible for keeping everyone alive, I knew that food was not a magical healing thing, that it could not bring my step-father back to life, that it could not make people feel better, could not fill the hollowness inside them. After all, it was just food. I was trapped between wanting to look after everyone and make it 'all right' and knowing that I could not do so, that they had to find ways of looking after themselves, and that all my cooking did not really help them very much at all, however much they thanked me and obediently ate what I produced. At the same time as feeling their lives depended on the meals I made, I also knew how pointless my efforts were, how little difference food made to the vast array of thoughts and feelings caused by a death.

One afternoon shortly after the funeral, we were all sitting in the garden and I offered to make sandwiches for everyone. 'No thank you darling,' my mother said. 'Oh come on, you must eat something.' 'Well, all right then, but not one of your doorstep sandwiches please.' I was mortified! It sounds such a trivial thing to mind about, but I was terribly upset by her unthinking slight. It was so important to me that I could do something useful, instead of giving in to my lurking feelings of total uselessness, and to discover I was doing it all wrong was unbearable. I was not upset about the thickness of my sandwiches, I was upset about the destruction of my already miniscule sense of my own worth.

It took me years to work out that behind my meal-making and desire to care for the others was a raging fear of my own emptiness and neediness. I was terrified of the great cavernous gaps inside me and had no idea how to begin to look after myself or care for myself. Instead I turned my attention away from myself and towards everyone else. The person I really wanted to keep alive, and the person I was most scared of failing to keep alive, was myself, but I didn't really know how to deal with that fear, so instead I ignored myself and concentrated – frantically – on meeting everyone else's needs. And the moments when I thought how useless I was at meeting the needs of others, such as when my mother rejected my doorstep sandwiches, were dreadful because underneath, inside, I knew it was my own needs I was failing to meet.

After my step-father's death I somehow convinced myself that if I gave in to my physical need (for food and all it represented: nurture, care, warmth, solidity, life), I would also be giving in to my emotional needs. That was an utterly terrifying prospect: I would be destroyed, obliterated by my own needs; they would well up inside me like a vast tidal wave and I would be swept away, drowned in their unstoppable flood. I had to keep a tight control of myself at all times, and the easiest way was through food. I must not give in to any of my needs, starting with the need for food. By determining to be thin and to get thinner, I was achieving two goals: first, by giving myself something else to think about, something other than all the pain and sorrow, something which was of my own making. I was at least taking control of something in my life, not like this dreadful business of death, imposed from the outside with no warning and no choice. Secondly, by not eating, I was able to tell the world how wretched I was, how frail and vulnerable and fragile. Even if I could hardly bear to see these things in myself, I still wanted to make everyone else see them.

So I got thinner and thinner. And when I went back to University in the autumn for my second year I had lost almost two stones. People were visibly shocked and openly solicitous. And secretly I was pleased. I would not let them forget what had happened to me; every time they looked at me I wanted them to think: 'Poor girl, her father and her step-father died'. I wanted them to feel sorry for me, to see that I was different, special, marked, cursed even, anything but normal, anything but like everyone else. I was determined that they should not expect me to be normal. I would not let them make me hide my feelings away behind a normal, healthy, happy facade. I wanted, I suppose, to punish them with my misery and make them realize how lucky they were. I was envious of their happiness and jealously guarded my right to unhappiness: I wanted them to feel guilty.

Being thin – and getting thinner – became an obsession and a cause, a crusade almost. It took up nearly all my thinking and energy for three or four years: planning how to eat, how to avoid eating, and how to pretend to eat. I took drugs to suppress my appetite which left me feeling depressed, so I took other drugs to suppress my depression. Some of these were supplied illegally by friends, others were supplied legally by my doctor. Sometimes I imagined I was winning the battle against grief, at other times it would submerge me. Mostly I wandered about in tears, feeling a complete and utter failure: I had failed to 'get over' my Dad's death, I was plainly failing to shut out my feelings about my step-father's death, and I had even failed as an anorexic! I was totally useless! I ended up very depressed, a combination of poor diet, drugs and, underlying everything, the great unavoidable grief that simply would not be ignored, no matter how hard I tried.

There is a Yiddish proverb which says, 'A man's worst enemy cannot wish him what he thinks up for himself.' Certainly the ways I devised to avoid the much feared pain of grief were still more frightening and more painful. Realizing this did not solve things overnight, but it marked a turning point. I still anaesthetized myself with food more often than I'd have liked, and I still panicked when uncomfortable feelings rose up inside me or when unexpected events happened, but increasingly I stopped setting myself against myself. I gradually stopped setting out to hurt myself, to attack myself. The day I realized that I was no longer using food to justify feeling miserable, but was instead using it now *in response* to feeling miserable was a real turning point.

Alcohol, drugs, sex and food can all be ways of shutting out the world, shutting out awareness of pain and sorrow, shutting out the knowledge of what has happened and the worry that it may happen again. The world is not a particularly safe place for the young. The risk of dying in a road accident, of being mugged or beaten up or of committing suicide is statistically higher in young people. A parent's death when you are in your teens and twenties can often feel like the final proof that being young is not all it is cracked up to be. You have a greater awareness of the gap which separates the idea of young people and the reality of being one. It is very easy and tempting to pretend to be as you think you ought to be, rather than plod along with painful reality. Drink, drugs and sex are all readily available accomplices in the crime of pretence. But the victim of the crime is usually yourself. They can make you believe you are young and OK, having fun, being normal, but usually their effect is only temporary and then you find yourself sucked into the trap of needing more of your fix to get you out of the low left by the last dose.

I messed myself up quite badly for a couple of years, took too many drugs and too many laxatives, too often dieted and binged, too often went to bed with people I felt too little for. None of it helped. In the short-term I was miserable and frightened by what I was doing, and in the long-term it didn't help me to deal with any of the underlying problems, whether they were linked or not to the two deaths which rocked my family and my life in and after 1981 and 1983. Maybe I simply could not have dealt with those problems any sooner, but I nevertheless regret having hurt myself so unnecessarily in those years before I *was* ready to deal with them.

Had there been more books on the subject, had the teachers at university been more clued up, had friends and relatives not been so scared themselves to see what was going on, had the counselling service been more available and more welcoming, I might not have had to wait so long. I wasn't up to helping myself, but had other people reached out to me I would have taken their proffered hands eventually. There were other people in the same position: none of us had much help or support other than what we could muster up for ourselves, which at that time was not a lot. The situation has improved a little in the last ten years, but not enormously. There is support out there but unfortunately the onus is still on you to go out and find it.

If you do feel that you are adding to your own pain and unhappiness, it may be some comfort just to tell yourself that: recognizing it is an important start. Try to be patient; wait for the moment – maybe still a couple of years away – when you will have the energy to help yourself, to go out and find what support you need, maybe a therapist or counsellor, maybe a lover, maybe an activity. Probably you will find you have more resources to help and heal yourself than at the moment you imagine. While you wait, try and tolerate the feelings and thoughts you have, without taking refuge in food, drink, drugs or another person's body. Try not to leap out of the frying pan and into the fire. Try instead to 'tolerate the wait', as a friend of mine in her eighties puts it. Learning to tolerate the wait, she says, is the only sure way through periods of intense pain, anguish, loneliness, uncertainty, fear, and disruption.

And while you wait, do try to protect yourself in non-destructive ways. A drink is not a bad thing, nor a piece of cake, nor physical affection. It is a matter of degree, and only you can know at what stage things stop being comforting and start to become dangerous. It is very easy to use other people as a shield against yourself when you are bereaved, when your own feelings and thoughts seem so frightening and destructive. It is easy to make the mistake of thinking that these feelings and thoughts are what should be avoided. But you can only deny yourself for so long without eventually damaging yourself. Whether your shield is other people's problems, drugs, drink, an older partner, a new country or an eating disorder, ultimately to remain healthy you will have to put down your shield and take a hard look at what is threatening you. Very often you will find nothing behind the shield. The thing you have been so frightened of is not behind the shield, but reflected in it. You have to face yourself and then start to look after that self. Ultimately no one else can do this for you, although they can help along the way. Try to be as honest with yourself as you can, don't think you are wrong or failing if you feel miserable at times. Try to tolerate the wait and be kind to yourself in the meantime.

10 Letting go and getting on

'The future is called "perhaps",
which is the only possible thing to call
the future. And the important thing
is not to allow that to scare you.'
(Tennessee Williams)

The previous chapters have explained how important it is both to understand the general nature of grief and to take into account the unique circumstances of your loss; how doing so makes it easier to accept how you are feeling and deal with it; how then in turn it becomes easier to understand and cope when future events in your life cause feelings of grief to recur with renewed force.

Sooner or later, however, the moment comes when you have to let go of grief and get on with your life as someone who *has been* bereaved rather than someone who *is* bereaved. This in no way invalidates the significance of your loss, or the continuing – and often painful – impact of that loss throughout your life. But it is a vital shift in perspective which marks the fact that life is happening for you once again in the fullest sense. Rushing into this before you are ready can be very harmful in the long run, but putting off indefinitely that moment of 'getting on' can be even more so.

231

At some point you will need to let go and get on. This is not always easy: some people find that grief has become a protective layer between them and the world and that over time they have actually grown dependent on the very condition they may hate; other people find grief 'useful', it lets them off the hook, becomes an easy fall-back when they don't feel up to the risks and challenges of life. Sometimes it is hard to know whether or not you are ready to let go of your pain and sorrow. Some people force themselves to get on with life before they have managed to let go – sometimes circumstances leave them no choice – and this is particularly a problem when you are young and so many other things are demanding your attention and energy. Sometimes you simply have to get on, and grieving has to wait. In that case the vital thing to remember, for reasons explained in the previous chapter, is that grieving has to be done at some point and there is a critical difference between delaying grief and trying to deny it.

For most people there will come a time when it is right to let go of your grief and get on with life. As Joyce Grenfell put it:

> Weep if you must
> Parting is hell
> But life goes on
> So sing as well
>
> (*Joyce, by Herself and Her Friends*)

This realization may come to you in a dream or in a flash of inspiration, it may come out of long and painful struggle perhaps in connection with a different situation or another person. For Debbie it came from a complete stranger.

Debbie's periods had stopped around the time of her mother's death and when after several years they still had not started again she began to worry. She hated this sign that she

232

was somehow not normal, not functioning properly. She had left home and moved to Leeds, living away from her family, in a responsible position at work, and channelled the anxiety she felt about these changes in her life into anxiety about her health. That year was a round of hospitals and doctors, being prodded, x-rayed, scanned and examined. It did nothing for her confidence or sense of well-being – although her anxiety thrived. The doctors could find nothing wrong. One suggested it was due to stress, but had nothing to say about how she should stop being stressed. Eventually Debbie decided to go and see a homeopathic doctor who listened carefully while she explained her symptoms, then gave her five minutes of straight talking.

'You have to let go of all this,' the doctor said. 'You have got to stop carrying all this bereavement around inside you. Your mother's not coming back. She's dead. You've got to get on with your life. Let go of her. You're a pretty girl. You've got enough money. You've got a good job. You're bright. You've got everything going for you. So stop this nonsense, let go of your mother and go out and get on with it.'

So much for the holistic approach! Debbie laughs now, to remember how amazed and angry she had been. How dare the doctor be so unsympathetic! How dare she be so impatient. 'But afterwards,' Debbie says, 'I realized her words had shaken something up inside me and maybe she was right. Maybe I was holding myself back. Maybe it was time to let go of it all. Accept that the dead are dead.' That was a turning point for Debbie. The doctor's words encouraged her to start letting go of her mother, to trust that she would not fade from her memory, and believe that it was safe to go into the future.

Her periods did gradually return after that, whether

233

because of the doctor's words or the workings of time, she doesn't know for sure. But what changed was her attitude: 'I decided to stop avoiding the future and try instead to get on with it. It was the first moment when I realized that I was the only one who could take the initiative for getting back into the mainstream of life.'

At a turning point in my own life, it was a dream that showed me how far I had come, how much had been achieved in this process of 'letting go and getting on' – although not without pain and wrong turnings and reversals. It was several years after my father and stepfather had died, and I had by then met the man I wanted to marry. The week we got engaged, I had a dream in which my father came in to the room, smiling at me, but without speaking, more an essence than a presence. I was overjoyed to see him and said, 'Oh, have you really come back then? Are you really here again?' As I said these words I was suffused with a feeling of warmth and safety and contentment. When I woke up, this sense of well-being stayed with me for a while. Before that I had not dreamt about my father for a very long time and it was as if, somehow, he had come now to give my marriage his blessing. For the first time since his death, I realized, I was allowing myself really to love someone again, to risk being hurt by him, to allow that element of risk back into my life, and therefore really to start living again. I won't say that from that moment onwards I lived happily ever after because it wouldn't be true, but I did and do feel that from that moment something still unresolved and unfinished in my relationship with my father and my reaction to his death, was sorted out, laid to rest so to speak.

• The fear of fear

Grieving in its early active stages involves reassessing the past and struggling with the present; the task now of squarely facing up to the future can be a daunting one. As Tennessee Williams knew, the future can seem a frightening place, full of risk and uncertainty and very often it is fear of the future as well as fear of the pain of grief that holds people back.

In an American comic routine called 'The Two Thousand Year Old Man', Mel Brooks plays the cranky, irrepressible two thousand year old man being interviewed about his life and times. The interviewer (Carl Reiner) asks him to explain the origin of song.

> 'The origin of song,' says the 2000 year old man, 'is fear.'
>
> 'Fear?' says the interviewer, very surprised.
>
> 'Yes, fear. You see a lion coming towards you, you say "help", no one hears you, the lion comes over and bites your leg off. Now, the next time you see a lion coming you YELL, at the top of your voice: "A LI-ON is BI-TING my LEG off. Will SOME-body CALL the COPS." *That* is how song began.'

The interviewer presses on:

> 'And, sir, can you tell us how dancing started? When did Man first begin to dance?'
>
> 'Well, that was fear too. A man has no eyes in the back of his head to see if a tiger or a lion's coming, so what does he do? He can't stand with his back to a tree all day long. So he asks another guy, preferably a lady, to watch over his shoulder for him. You over mine and me over yours. See! Left a little. Right a little. You got dancing!'
>
> 'It seems, sir,' says the interviewer, 'that most things stemmed from fear. Is that right?'
>
> 'Yes. Mostly from fear. Yes.'

To stay alive, people must be prepared to feel fearful sometimes, but not to be ruled by fearfulness. After someone dies the temptation to avoid fear at all costs is very great. But being frightened is not a bad thing in itself; it is not wrong or shameful to be frightened. It is when you begin to fear fear itself, become frightened of being frightened, that the problems begin. You may fear dissolution, chaos and collapse, but knowing what you are afraid of creates the possibility of their very opposite: growth, revival, strength.

It may seem hard to believe, but fear is not the enemy: it is in fact a vital part of yourself and your life – in the original sense of the word 'vital', meaning 'of life'. And that is the paradoxical thing about fear, it can be either vital or deadly, it has the capacity either to keep us alive or to cut us off from the source of life. The child who knows no fear will put a hand into the fire. Knowing what is safe and what is dangerous, knowing what to trust and what to fear, saves your life every day in all sorts of ways. Fear of death and dying, Rousseau maintained over two hundred years ago, 'is the great law of sentient beings, without which the entire human species would soon be destroyed'.

But fear is not wholly positive: if the human being who discovered fire had concluded after the first time he or she got burnt that fire was to be feared and avoided altogether the human species might well have died of cold and never made it to the twentieth century. Fear can make you turn your back on things you need, such as human warmth, it can make you shun the uncontrolledness of loving another person. It can make you turn your back on the world, avoid changes and challenges, avoid any situation which might be in any way difficult or dangerous or risky.

I know people who have turned their backs on life through fear. On the outside they seem fine. Maybe they do have nice flats or well-paid jobs or endless streams of girlfriends, but something in them has stopped nevertheless. They create a dangerous kind of control in their lives in order never to feel the fear of being out of control. They won't leave their jobs even though they hate them and don't need the money. They never stay with a partner longer than a few weeks. They can't stand having visitors in their lovely homes. Maybe they drink too much or smoke too much. Maybe they take laxatives at night to control their weight or live at the pub rather than face an evening alone. I also know people who have simply withdrawn from the world altogether, who do not go out, do not have friends, do not risk anything. Like the hypothetical first human being, who would never risk being burnt, they too are slowly freezing from lack of warmth.

According to St Thomas: 'If you bring forth what is inside you, what you bring forth will save you.' The most frightening things are the things inside your own heart and mind. If you dare to look at them and know them and get them out of the darkness into the light you will be all the stronger for it. It is the fear of fear that stops you looking at or 'bringing forth' what is inside you; that is the real risk, the real danger, the real thing to be wary of. Fear itself is useful: it tells you about yourself. Not much in life is worse than the things in yourself that you fear and having once looked at them, nothing else is ever so scary again.

It took me a long, long time to stop fighting (and at the same time denying) my fear, and instead to give it a little room to be. When I found I could do that, I realized that things were not so threatening and dreadful after all. Alongside the fear and despair, I realized, there was also determination and hopefulness. Looking back it makes me very sad to see how

237

hard I was on myself. My whole life at that time was a kind of war against myself, a frantic haze of activity which attacked, and I hoped would subdue, the great army inside me. I was like a person besieged, trapped inside myself. And at the same time I was the besieger, the one doing the trapping. I didn't know if I was inside trying to get out, or outside trying to get in. So I just kept building the walls of my battlements and trying to find chinks and holes in the walls – whether to block up or peer through, I didn't know.

But I did know really. At the end of the day, I knew, there was no difference: sooner or later I would have to face all the things I didn't want to face. I would have to accept responsibility for myself – and all that involved: allowing myself to be *not* in control, accepting that the world was bigger than me and there were things in it I could do nothing about, things that I could only hope to find ways of dealing with, but never ways of causing or preventing. What I slowly, gradually realized was that I was in some ways helpless and powerless, that there were things outside and inside myself that I could not have control over. I just had to let things be, the things I liked and wanted and wished for *and* the things I dreaded and hated and feared. I had to take what there was and work *with* that, not against it.

• Taking responsibility for yourself

Trying to avoid painful feelings – or maybe just all feelings – is no way to live: feelings are only avoidable at huge cost to yourself. You *can*, if you wish, choose to avoid feelings and risk the long-term consequences of that. Or you can try to accept that feelings are not good or bad, though they may be pleasant or painful: feelings just *are*. If you want to continue in the world leading a fulfilled life, then feelings will *be*. This is not a decision made overnight that will instantly illumine your life; it is a way of being, taken in small steps each time you reach a crossroads in your life when you have choice about which path to take.

There are many, many crossroads at which you can exercise choice over your life and yourself. Even when you are convinced you are at a dead-end not a crossroads, it is worth remembering a Yiddish proverb: 'No choice is a choice.' Leaving home, starting a new job, moving house, sitting exams: any major event in your life, any event that feels important to you, will nearly always have somewhere about it a crossroads, an element of choice.

Basically there are just two roads to choose between: one marked 'The Adult World' and the other marked 'Childhood'. The other two branches of the signpost say 'Circular Route' and 'Cliff Edge'. If you can't make a choice between the adult route and the childhood one, then the circular route is the next-best option. It is a safe path because it allows you to do something while ultimately bringing you back to where you started. But the other, the one marked 'Cliff Edge', is often the more tempting route, particularly when you may be feeling scared and confused, and panicking about how to proceed. It seems to offer a short cut to where you want to go, or sometimes a completely different destination from the one you should be heading for. This route seems attractive, fascinating, exciting, easy. It is the route you take when you start taking drugs in the months leading up to important exams. It is the route you take when you fail to turn up for an interview. Or drop out of college after three weeks. It is the route which ultimately leads to a worse situation than the one you hoped to leave behind, the route which becomes more frightening the further along it you go. In the end it is a route that tends to bring you up against nothing more substantial than thin air. All your ideas about where this route might have led have instead led to this: nothingness, just you and the cliff edge.

Nevertheless it is the route people often take when hounded by complicated emotions, when pursued, and even persecuted, by the constant need to make choices at a time when you simply don't feel up to it. Choice is a pain. It involves responsibility, and at the age of sixteen, eighteen or twenty-two, responsibility is the last thing you need. Responsibility is like a mammoth round your neck, never mind an albatross. If choice is a pain, responsibility is even more of a pain. It demands thought and attention. It demands that you look at yourself, your situation, your future, all of which can be fearful things to look at when you are still shaken by a parent's death. Responsibility can be particularly awesome in these circumstances because the person who died was the very one you supposed would be around to take that responsibility, to make those choices for you. Responsibility adds insult to the injury of death.

Sometimes I used to wail to myself: 'I don't want to be mature and grown-up. I'm not ready. Leave me alone.' I felt as if I had been hauled out of adolescence where I had been quite happy, thank you, and given altogether a raw deal. 'I don't want responsibility,' I'd yell silently to no one in particular, 'I don't want it. Somebody else is supposed to do that stuff.' I would look at my schoolfriends, and later on my college friends, and think how easy life seemed for them. In my most uncharitable moments I'd catch myself thinking: 'You wait. It'll happen to you sooner or later, and then you'll know how dreadful it is having to grow up too soon.' But of course the key injustice is that if a parent dies when you are in your thirties or forties, it may be hard but in many ways you will by then be grown-up. You will have had time to get used to making decisions for yourself, and taking responsibility for your life. Not everyone does, of course. I have heard men in their sixties say they have only just grown up now with their parent's death, but at least they have had some practice at it. In your teens and twenties, you may still have had no real responsibilities for ourself or for the direction your life will take. Other people pay the mortgage, rent, electricity, car insurance. Other people buy the food, replace the loo paper, empty the bins. Other people collect up your coffee cups and wash your sheets. It is therefore especially shocking suddenly to have to take this degree of responsibility for yourself, and at a time when so few of your friends have to. They continue, blissfully, blithely, as before, while all the brightness goes out of your life, and you find it is now all problems, worries, anxieties, decisions – things you had not imagined having to deal with for maybe another ten years.

One of the hardest lessons of bereavement that I learned was that no one in the world was more responsible for me than I was for myself. People cared for me and loved me and helped me, but no one else was responsible for me. Much as you too might want to eschew that responsibility, in the end it is yours, and you have to own it. Sometimes fully accepting the fact of that responsibility for yourself can come as a relief. It can give you a sense of power, of authority, of having effect. It is a

241

position from which you can look after yourself, value yourself, give yourself what you need.

But when it is foisted on you prematurely, it can take a long time to feel and see the good aspects of this responsibility. It is like being made to wear an overcoat – a very thick, heavy overcoat, which is five sizes too big. It gets in the way. It hangs around your heels and trips you up. It drags over your hands and drops in your food. It is uncomfortable and cumbersome. It slows you down. It makes it impossible to move quickly and easily. Eventually, however, you find it fits a bit better: you can roll back the cuffs if necessary, you can move around in it after all, it keeps you warm, protects you from the cold and damp. Inside your coat you find you are in fact a good deal safer than you were without it. Eventually you even find it is possible to take it off and hang it up for a while.

After a parent's death, you may have to cope with considerable responsibility for other people as well as for yourself. Any kind of responsibility can then feel like a vast unwanted weight about your neck.

The mantle of self-responsibility is an annoying garment that sits not at all easily at first, but it gets easier to bear. Once you can accept it, responsibility for yourself can bring with it a tremendous sense of relief and of freedom: you are in charge, you are not a powerless child to whom things happen without warning, you are an adult who can respond to the vicissitudes of fortune in ways that will be good for you. You are free to live your life according to your own needs.

• The power of memory

If learning to live with fear and accepting responsibility for yourself are two crucial steps towards 'letting go', a third is recognizing the importance of remembering. Getting on with your life does not mean you must forget all about the past, but rather that you must discover a place for the past in the future. This may sound contradictory, but it is expressed beautifully in a passage from the novel, *Dr Zhivago*. Yuri tells Anna, who is dying, that her death will not be the end of her existence: 'You have always been in others and you will remain in others,' he says. 'And what does it matter to you if later on it is called your memory? This will be you – the real you that enters the future and becomes a part of it.'

To take this idea on board involves a radical shift in thinking, because most of us are used to regarding death as an end, a full stop; even if you believe in some form of life after death it is still hard to feel that you have any connection with the person who has died.

Eight months after my father's death, I wrote in my diary:

It's as if only now have I come to realize the difference between 'dead' and 'away'. I miss Dad so much. Not just as sadness, but as an enormous anger. I feel angry, angry, angry – that I shall never know him, nor he me. And I feel angry that I wasted the last years of his life with my friends, instead of with him. All the memories I have of Dad are spoiled with regret, bitterness, guilt. Even three more years and I might have come to know him a little. It makes me so sad and angry. I so want to know him, and I can't. It's just not fair. That's what I feel – like a spoilt child who can't have what she wants. I miss him so much and often I find myself on the verge of tears. If only, only, only there'd been time to know him a bit.

This feeling of having been cheated is common after someone dies, particularly a parent who has died when you are both still relatively young. I have heard plenty of people utter this

243

complaint: that someone and something has been taken away unfairly, the rules of the game have been changed without any warning, the goalposts moved while your back was turned.

What has been taken away is not just a person you needed to be alive still, but also time. Time to do your own thing, time to get to know your parent as a person, time to fight and make up with your family, time to get away from them for long enough to get to know yourself a bit, time to be young and carefree, time to be selfish and independent.

When someone you care about goes on holiday for a couple of weeks, you expect to miss that person, you accept that you will think about and talk about her or him. But when someone you care about dies, there is an unspoken assumption that that person will be erased from your life. Not just from your life now, but your life in the past and in the future. So the voices in your head tell you, and the voices you imagine are in other people's heads. But it is a great mistake to listen to these voices. Forget about other people, the only person who really matters is you, and most probably you will want and need to carry on thinking and talking about your parent.

Your parent has not vanished, he or she is still with you in your memory, in your attitudes, in your likes and dislikes. The worst thing you can do for yourself is to pretend that nothing has happened, that you are not affected. The best thing you can do is give yourself as much time as you need to get used to the idea that they are dead and to the idea that you must now form a new kind of relationship with them.

It will not feel so at first, perhaps not for several years, but eventually there can come a point when you will begin to discover that the time you feel so cheated of is there after all. This is a monumental discovery: there *is* time! Not the kind of time you expected to have, but time nevertheless. You *can* have a relationship with someone who has died. In exactly the same way as a person who goes away continues to be alive in your memory, so a parent who has died does. There is not the same possibility for reunion, but neither is there the absolute halt to your relationship that you might in the early days have supposed.

In the first few years after my father's death, I had the disturbing experience of somehow having him in me, of carrying him in an almost physical sense inside me, so that at times it was as if I were 'being him'. I would catch myself sitting in the same way my father used to, or walking in the same way. It was as if I were doing those things for him now that he could no longer do them for himself. I found this sensation of 'being him' odd and unsettling. His presence inside me was sad and burdensome, as well as wanted. But as the years have passed, this sense of him as a physical presence has worn off; I no longer feel I have to carry him inside me in order to keep him alive, but can find comfort from the memory of him inside me instead. I can still be close to him, still be my father's daughter; it is no longer a burdensome presence inside me, but rather a comfortable space, like a little private meeting place to go to when I want to be with him.

To find this comfortable – and comforting – room for the past has taken many years. For at least the first two or three years, I was not at all able to feel positive about Dad's death: eight months after his death I was still suffering from violent outbursts of grief and anger that would take hold of me without warning, often in the most incongruous situations.

245

One day, for instance, I was cleaning the bath and suddenly I was overcome with grief and pain and sobbing my heart out. This incident upset me: I was shocked to find so much raw emotion still lurking such a little way beneath the surface. Nowadays I am not afraid of the sudden memories that come to me in unexpected moments, the wave of 'Oh, oh, oh, why isn't he alive still?'. I can allow these waves of sadness and regret to wash in, take hold for a while, knowing from experience that they will eventually subside again.

Before you can live with memories you have to look at them, you have to allow yourself to have them. This is easier to understand in the context of a physical memento of the person, such as a piece of their clothing or a photograph. There was a photograph of my father I was particularly fond of. It showed a side of him I loved: on holiday in a café with a glass of something good to drink in one hand and a spoonful of something good to eat in the other and a huge smile all over his face. This was the fun-loving, good-living, joke-cracking father I had adored. In the months immediately after his death I used to gaze at it and long for him to be alive again. Sometimes I would wonder bitterly if it was the good living that had killed him. But whether the picture roused sad or angry feelings, I was glad to have it there, to be able to see his face.

Later on I went through a stage of wondering if it was wrong to have the photograph of a dead man on my pinboard, perhaps it was morbid. For a while I put it away. The one day I came across it again, and the lovely expression on my father's face reminded me how infectious his happiness had been and how much I had loved his company at such times: I decided to put it back on my pinboard. I don't *need* it in the way I once did, but I no longer think about taking it down. I no longer feel ashamed of wanting to remember him at times. My father is still part of me and so why pretend otherwise? There are photos of other people who matter to me on the board, so why not him who has mattered and does matter more than most? Sometimes I see the photo and it makes me sad, sometimes it makes me smile, mostly it just gives me a small quiet sense that he is around still somewhere, if nowhere else then in my memory.

You are entitled to your past and to your memories. Unless they are making you ill or destroying you in some way, no one should take them away from you. A sense of the past gives a sense of continuity and a sense of purpose, knowing where you came from affirms your sense of what and where you are now. And knowing where you came from and where you are now in turn enables you to go on into the future. Too much past is a bad thing, but no past at all is possibly worse. To deny what you have been, have had, have done, and have had done to you, is to deny the importance and significance of your experience, of your life, of *you*. A bit of past is a very precious thing and beware of anyone who says otherwise. A bit of past and the ability to value the past and value memory not only gives your life meaning, it also gives meaning to the lives of those who have died.

There is another Yiddish saying that seems relevant here: 'Considering how little your parents know when you are fifteen, it's amazing what they have learnt by the time you reach thirty.'

It is not your parents who have changed, but you, and as you change, your perspective on the world, on yourself and on your parents changes too. This is so whether they are alive or dead.

Even after their death, you will get to know them differently as with time and experience you change; and through you, they too will have the capacity to change with time.

Daniel is in his late fifties, a university lecturer, married with four children. His father died when he was fourteen and obviously his feelings about his father's death have changed as he has got older, as the years have passed and wedged themselves between him and his original loss. His feelings now are different, he says, but not necessarily easier. 'In a funny way I miss Dad *more* now. I am more aware of not sharing things with him. The events in my life that I would have liked to share with him accumulate over time, and each one reminds you. Having sons of my own completely changed my view of my father. But the strangest thing of all was reaching the age he'd been when he died: that makes you realize something new about how they must have been in the world. I am now eighteen years *older* than my father. I have passed him in age – and that is really weird. No, his death doesn't get easier with time, it just changes. You never forget, because there are always more things to remind you!'

Discovering new things about your relationship with a person who has died and discovering more about the kind of person they were – and could have been for you had they lived – takes time and is often a painful process, but it does allow your parent to live on through you in a way which is, ultimately, profoundly life-affirming for them and, more importantly, for you. 'There is no death, daughter. People die only when we forget them,' the dying mother says to her daughter in the novel *Eva Luna*. 'If you can remember me, I will be with you always.'

'I will remember,' the daughter promises.

248

At the beginning of this book I emphasized the uniqueness of your relationship with the person who died, something composed of the particular mixture of your two personalities, something that no one else can ever fully understand because it is something only you and your parent experienced. It is important to acknowledge that to yourself in the early days of a bereavement. It is equally important to recognize it later on when you are ready to start living again. Your unique relationship with your parent may be a source of deep pain or a source of joy, probably a mixture of the two; what matters is allowing yourself to remember. Refusing to remember, killing your past, at some level kills you too. To live again, you must also let your dead live, and to do that you must let them stretch and breathe in your memory.

I find now I can remember my father without being frightened. I can share my memories with him. I can watch how my sense of who he was and who I was then has changed with time. I can enjoy thinking about him. I remember a man who sent me a postcard every morning of my A levels, one of a different famous author each day to arrive before I set off to school: Jane Austen, George Eliot, Keats, Shelley and Thomas Hardy. I remember a man who always sent me wonderful birthday cards – my birthday always fell during termtime – and lovely postcards from his holidays in Italy. One of the last was of a fresco of a couple in the bath. On the back of the card he'd written 'Saving water can be fun!' That was typical of a side of my father I loved. It was the same friskiness that often brought on impromptu ditties as we were walking down the street together. Sometimes he might even skip a little!

I remember a man who spent infinite care wrapping paper,

249

ribbons and bows until the whole thing looked like a work of art; a man who understood that a little girl appreciates a Christian Dior handkerchief in her Christmas stocking even before she knows who Christian Dior is. A man who adored opera and would sing along to *The Magic Flute* or *Don Giovanni* lustily and tunelessly; a man who enjoyed good food and wine, who on the one hand would buy Tip Tree conserve for himself and Robertson's jam for the children, but on the other hand would give me a sip of a first-class claret so that I might enjoy it too. Going round delicatessens with him was a joy, and nothing compared with his love of a good French patisserie. On camping holidays in Normandy, I just adored the look of guilty delight on his face as he appeared round a corner in some village with a little ribboned box swinging from his hand.

I remember too a man who had a fondness for cashmere socks and who regularly polished the kitchen floor with them, one toe delicately outstreched like a ballerina's; who made the best macaroni cheese in the world, which in my step-mother's absence we would improve still further with lashings of tomato ketchup. Our other culinary game was making Smash instant potato. The challenge was to make it edible by throwing in whatever we could think of: vinegar, paprika, ketchup, eggs, butter, curry powder. We'd usually eaten most of it in the tasting process before the final product reached the table.

I remember a man with a deep appreciation of art, music and literature, which I had little time for at that stage. I remember often seeing him stretched out on the sofa with a whisky and a volume of Keats or Shelley balanced on his chest. I remember so fondly the man who, for my eighteenth birthday, decided it was high time I learned a bit about classical music. Once a fortnight a record would arrive

250

through the post of some major musical work by Schubert, Mozart, Beethoven or Vivaldi. I see now a man who realized how hard it is to start learning these things–and so he got on and started me! The last record–Beethoven's violin concerto–arrived ten days before he died.

I remember too with ever-increasing gratitude a man who took me to Rome when I was sixteen and brought the whole city, past and present, alive for me. It was the last holiday we went on together. I think one of the few times in my life that I have been stunned into silence was when Dad took me round the ruins of the Forum under a baking Roman sun and somehow made the crumbling walls and half-buried foundations rise out of the dust to all their former magnificence. In the art galleries he showed me how to look at the Giottos and Botticellis. In the cafés he taught me how to sit and watch the world. We got up early to reach the Sistine Chapel before the crowds; we threw coins into the Trevi Fountain, and one night we got lost in the red-light district coming back from a restaurant.

I think I always knew about the sadness in my father, the deep fears and anxieties, but it is through these memories that I have gradually discovered also a man who possessed a tremendous capacity for fun and a tremendous gift for sharing his enjoyment. I have got to know my father better in the ten years since his death, perhaps better than I could have done had he lived. In ways like this, I realize, something very positive can come out of death.

You too will have your memories of this most special of relationships, both the good sides of it and the bad. Hang on to them. You are the keeper of the past and your memories are the keys to the future.

251

• Letting go and getting on

Grieving is hard work, but so is letting go of grief and getting on with life. To do so you have to find the courage to face the three most frightening things of all: mortality, your own self and the uncertainty of tomorrow. Letting go of grief means overcoming the fear of fear; looking your loss in the face and accepting it, and learning to love your memories not shun them. Getting on with life means accepting that your childhood is over; taking responsibility for yourself, accepting both control of your life and lack of it, and finally–paradoxically–it means allowing the dead to live on in your memory. Your parent, alive and dead, remains an integral part of your life then, now and in the future, not a chunk of your past to be severed and strewn by the wayside of your sorrow.

There is a saying in the City about not following a bad share. In other words, when something is over, let it go and get on with the next thing. When parents die you have to do exactly this. You have to let go of them and let go of the pain of losing them–not immediately, but eventually. You must give yourself time to think about them, mourn for them, hate them for dying, rage at them for leaving you–and then you have to accept that they live now not in the world but in your memory; rather than looking backwards over your shoulder at the past, you must go with your memories into the future.

I have learnt a great deal about myself in the process of learning to live with a parent's death. Not all of it is particularly nice, but it is useful nevertheless. I can see, for instance, how I threw myself into wholly unsuitable relationships and would then be inconsolable when the inevitable break-up came, how I used these hopeless affairs to express the grief and despair I was afraid to feel directly in relation to their real source. I can see how my fear of loss and my fear of my own rage at being 'left' by the deaths of my father and step-father pushed me not just into men's arms, but into jobs and friendships that had little to do with what I liked, needed or wanted. I did so many things simply to avoid feelings that I was scared of, or because they seemed to be safer causes of distressing feelings than the vast incomprehensible impact of death. I don't exactly regret my mistakes because in a way I had to do the wrong things often enough to *make* myself see that I was doing them wrong, to *convince* me that I ought to try a different approach. I don't think I wasted my time in the last ten years, but I certainly took plenty of it to get to a stage where I feel reasonably confident that I can let my past be, live equably in the present, anticipate enjoyment of the future and have the strength to deal with the inevitable troubles and tragedies the future holds. I feel able to believe the Jewish proverb that says: 'He that can't endure the bad, will not live to see the good.' I know that both good and bad, happiness and sorrow lie ahead—and that in all probability they will be endurable.

11   Last words

'Death is nothing at all . . .
I have only slipped away into the
next room . . .
I am I and you are you . . .
Whatever we were to each other
that we are still.'
(Henry Scott Holland)

Coming back on the train from London to Oxford one evening earlier this year after an enjoyable evening with a gentleman in his late seventies, an old family friend of my fiancé's, I was overwhelmed suddenly with sadness and longing for my father, and reminded once again how the effects of death continue to make themselves felt long, long after the event; reminded once again that however much sense I have managed to make of my father's death, still there is a part of my heart and brain that simply cannot comprehend that he is dead.

It has taken all of ten years to find ways of coping, of putting death in its place, of being able to engage in life, of being able to hope for and anticipate without dread what tomorrow will bring. I still miss my father terribly at times, particularly at times of change when I realize he is not able to share these important moments with me. He will never meet my husband, nor my children. A few weeks ago my oldest brother, now thirty-three, sent me a photograph of himself, his five month old son, Ben, and our grandfather, Mark, who is in his eighties. Three generations: eighty-eight, thirty-three and five months. The family likeness was very strong, even in the baby. *Already* in the baby! But the photograph made me sad, even as it made me smile, because the absence of one face was so obvious, the missing person so unmissable. There should have been another generation sitting there on the sofa smiling at the camera.

The death of a parent, I have learned, is not something that fades with time. The person and the sadness of his or her death and the pain of your loss are changed by the years, as you are yourself, but they stay with you all the same. Nothing is untouched by time, but the expression 'time is a great healer' is misleading: time is not so much a great healer as a great transformer. The Christian funeral liturgy emphasizes this with the words, 'earth to earth, ashes to ashes, dust to dust', life is changed, life is not taken away. For some the transformation will be relatively quick and smooth, for others it is a long and painful process. Whatever happens, time cannot erase your loss, but neither will it leave your grief unchanged.

Writing this book has made me reach into recesses of myself I would perhaps rather have left untouched. My sorrow is there still, just as much as the fact of my father's death is there still, but the last ten years have seen changes and transformations too. Sorrow does not interfere so much now with living; the impact of death has come to show some positive elements, not just the negative ones I felt at the beginning. Being aware of the nearness of death to life has made me better able to appreciate and value the preciousness of the moment. Perhaps most surprisingly I have evolved ways of having my father in my life with me, I am not conscious of it most of the time, but nevertheless he is there. Coming to terms with death in general, as well as the specific deaths of people I have loved, has made me if not more willing to take risks, then certainly more aware of the necessity of risk-taking in life, more ready to acccpt that life is risk, that living is about taking risks, about 'daring to become', or as the theologian Paul Tillich put it, having 'the courage to be'.

Shortly before I finished this book a friend asked if I had found writing it a useful experience. I knew what he was getting at, but I had to be honest: this has been a painful book to write. It has meant overriding all the methods I had so carefully developed over the last ten years to protect myself; it has meant dismissing the strategies I had devised to make some sense of death and tame the beast of grief. Writing this book has made it necessary to go once more to the source of grief and re-experience feelings I had hoped not to feel again: sorrow, fear, pain, anger, confusion. Whether it has been a *useful* exercise for me, I need a little more time between the writing of it and the assessing of it to be able to tell. Whether or not I found writing this book a useful experience is in a way irrelevant: what I do know is that I wanted to write the kind of book that was not around when my father and step-father died, the kind of book I badly needed, that would have made me feel less alone, less scared, less abandoned. I have written this book in the hope that it might go some way to ease the lonely suffering of other teenagers and young adults in the aftermath of a parent's death. If even one person in the course of reading this book says: 'Yes! I feel just like that,' then it will without doubt have been worthwhile.

Death is out there, waiting for each one of us. But that realization need not be oppressive and threatening; instead it can release us into the very heart of living. The process of accepting that death is inevitable, that sorrow and pain are equally inevitable, that plans will fall through, that the unexpected will happen, that events and feelings are not always within our control—these realizations can come as a relief. For given those things, what can we do but throw ourselves into the business of life: hopes, joys, uncertainties, upsets, delight, sorrow and all? There is no choice: we must in the end dare to go on.

If nothing else my encounters with death have taught me this: that we will die and those we love will die. That thorny fact remains, as yet, unsolved by science, it gives meaning to our endeavours and it renders our endeavours meaningless, and in the meantime we must get on with what is both the simplest and the most awesome of tasks: we must dare to live.

Suggested reading

• Books on bereavement

Bereavement by Christopher Golding (Crowood Press, 1991). Useful chapters on the death of a parent, the death of a baby, and the practical aspects of bereavement.

Bereavement by Colin Murray Parkes (Tavistock, 1972). Aimed primarily at carers, but worth reading if you wish to know more about the subject of bereavement in general.

Care of the dying by Dame Cicely Saunders (Macmillan, 1959); **Coping with a dying relative** by Derek Doyle (Macdonald, 1984); **The hospice way** by D. Winn (Macdonald Optima, 1987).
Three books that offer support for those caring for someone with a terminal illness, and provide useful information about hospices.

Coping with bereavement by Sandra Horn (Thorsons, 1989). Good chapters on the funeral, the practical aspects of grief, and the loss of a baby or child, through abortion, miscarriage and stillbirths.

Coping with suicide by Ronald Scott (Sheldon Press, 1991). Tackles the issues facing people bereaved by suicide with compassion and understanding.

The courage to live by Dorothy Rowe (Fontana, 1991). Explores the difficulties and the importance of accepting and living with death.

Death and the family: the importance of mourning by Lily Pincus (Faber & Faber, 1976). Primarily for widows and widowers, but very good on how people grieve in different ways.

Facing grief – bereavement and the young adult by Susan Wallbank (Lutterworth Press, 1991). One of the few books around written specifically for young people, this has particularly good sections on the differing effects of a mother's or a father's death.

Grief – the play, writings and workshops by Penny Casdagli and Francis Gobey, with Caroline Griffin (David Fulton, 1992). Based on the play by the Neti-Neti Theatre Company, this book includes the script of the play itself, together with writing by young people and professionals. For information about the play and copies of the script, contact 44 Galdsmuir Road, London N19 8JU; tel. 071-272 7302. A video of **Grief** is also available from the same address, for £49.95.

Grief counselling and grief therapy by J. William Worden (Tavistock, 1983). A text-book for carers, but also helpful to the bereaved.

Grief in children by Atle Dyregrov (Jessica Kingsley, 1990).

A grief observed by C.S. Lewis (Faber & Faber, 1978). Autobiographical account of the writer's thoughts and feelings after his wife's death. Sensitive and accessible.

How it feels when a parent dies edited by J. Krementz (Gollancz, 1986). Accounts by eighteen children of different ages of how they experienced a parent's death.

I never told her I loved her by Sandra Chick (Livewire Books, 1989). A novel about a teenager coping with her mother's death and her new role as 'woman of the house'.

Merely mortal – coping with dying, death and bereavement by Sarah Boston and Rachael Trezise (Methuen, 1987). Personal accounts of grief and general discussion about death, mortality

Suggested reading

and loss. Chapter 7 is excellent on practical and legal procedures when someone has died, taking you through every stage.

On death and dying by Elisabeth Kubler-Ross (Tavistock, 1970). Particularly useful for people coping with a death from terminal illness.

The secret garden by Frances Hodgson Burnett (Puffin, 1911). Classic children's book about two bereaved children finding friendship and renewed faith in life.

A very easy death by Simone de Beauvoir (Penguin, 1969). A frank and moving account of her mother's death.

• Practical books

The following books offer information and guidelines for coping with the practical, legal and medical aspects of a bereavement.

Faith and practice – a guide to Reform Judaism today by Jonathan Romain (Reform Synagogues of Great Britain, 1991). Outlines the funeral rites and mourning rituals in Reform Judaism today. Clear and accessible.

Funerals – and how to improve them by Dr Tony Walters (Hodder & Stoughton, 1990). Includes practical information, ideas and advice about the practice and organization of funerals.

Funerals without God: a practical guide to non-religious funerals by Jane Wynne Willson (British Humanist Association, 1989). An excellent guide for anyone wanting an alternative to a religious service.

261

Help when someone dies, Form FB29 from Department of Social Security. Leaflet on social security benefits available.

What to do after a death, Form D49 from Department of Social Security. Leaflet explaining the practical procedure and requirements.

What to do when someone dies by the Consumers' Association (Hodder & Stoughton, 1986). Contains practical and legal information.

• Books on depression

Depression – the way out of your prison by Dorothy Rowe (Routledge, 1989). Offers a compassionate understanding of depression and invaluable insights into coping with it.

Beyond fear (Fontana, 1987) also by Dorothy Rowe and equally inspiring.

Images of destruction by David Wigoder (Routledge Kegan Paul, 1987). One man's account of his descent into suicidal depression and gradual journey towards an understanding of his experience and renewed hope in the future. Very useful for anyone struggling with emotional confusion – their own or a relative's.

• Books on compulsive behaviour

The Casanova complex: compulsive lovers and their women by Peter Trachtenbergy (Eden Paperbacks). Explains how relationships can become a vehicle of aggression against others and oneself.

The complete guide to psychiatric drugs by Ron Lacey (Elbury Press, 1991). A handbook for the lay person outlining the risks, side-effects, hazards and possible benefits of psychiatric drugs. Important for anyone taking or planning to take them.

Escape from tranquillizers and sleeping pills by Larry Nield (Ebury Press, 1990). A DIY withdrawal plan for anyone caught in the tranquillizer trap, by the co-founder of Tranxline.

Fat is a feminist issue by Susie Orbach (Arrow Books, 1984). **Hunger strike** by Susie Orbach (Faber and Faber, 1986). Two books that will be invaluable for anyone struggling with eating problems. Sensible and sympathetic.

I'll quit tomorrow by Vernon E. Johnson (Harper & Row). A practical guide to alcoholism treatment.

Quit compulsive gambling by Gordon Moody (Thorsons). A self-help book for those held in the grip of gambling.

Womansize: the tyranny of slenderness by Kim Chernin (The Women's Press, 1983). Personal account of the author's struggle with compulsive eating and bulimia; explains why and how food and weight become weapons used against the self.

Women's secret disorder–a new understanding of bulimia by Mira Dana and Marilyn Lawrence (Grafton Press, 1988). A useful book for those trapped in the binge-diet cycle.

• Other useful books

Families and how to survive them by Robin Skynner and John Cleese (Mandarin Paperbacks, 1990). An invaluable read for anyone wanting to understand how relationships within families have implications for the rest of your life.

The trauma of moving by Audrey T. McCollum (Sage Publications, 1990). Very useful for anyone interested in understanding why moving can be so painful.

When a woman's body says no to sex by Linda Valins (Penguin, 1992). Explains the physical, emotional and psychological causes of vaginismus, and offers practical advice for overcoming it.

Useful organizations

BEREAVEMENT TRUST
Stanford Hall
Loughborough
Leicestershire LE12 5QR
Tel: 0509 852333
Provides information about bereavement support services across the country.

CANCERLINK
46 Pentonville Road
London N1 9HF
Tel: 071-833 2451
Has an information service to provide support and advice to people with cancer, their families and friends.

COT DEATH SOCIETY
1 Mansell Drive
Wash Common, Newbury
Berkshire RG14 6TE
Tel: 0635 523756
Provides support for bereaved parents of cot-death babies.

CRUSE–BEREAVEMENT CARE
126 Sheen Road, Richmond
Surrey TW9 1UR
Tel: 081-940 4818
Groups throughout the country, mostly for widowed spouses and parents, but also some for young people. Also offer counselling to all bereaved.

FOUNDATION FOR BLACK BEREAVED FAMILIES
11 Kingston Square
Salters Hill
London SE19 1JE
Tel: 081-661 7228
Provides support and advice to bereaved black families across the country.

FOUNDATION FOR THE STUDY OF INFANT DEATHS
35 Belgrave Square
London SW1X 8PS
Tel: 071-235 0965
Provides support and information to parents of cot-death babies.

THE GAY BEREAVEMENT PROJECT
c/o Gay Switchboard
Tel: 071-837 7324 (24 hours)
Based in London, but can offer contacts for other parts of the country.

HOSPICE INFORMATION SERVICE
51-59 Lawrie Park Road
Sydenham, London SE26 6DZ
Tel: 081-778 1240
Can send a *Directory of Hospice Services* with details of hospices in your area and information on other kinds of terminal care available. (Your GP, local Citizens' Advice Bureaux and Social Services offices should also have this information.)

INSTITUTE OF FAMILY THERAPY
43 New Cavendish Street
London W1M 7RG
The Elizabeth Raven Memorial Fund offers free counselling to newly bereaved families or those with terminally ill family members.

THE JEWISH BEREAVEMENT COUNSELLING SERVICE
1 Cyprus Gardens
London N3 1SP
Tel: 071-349 0839
Provides emotional support and help and information about Jewish bereavement rituals and customs.

THE MISCARRIAGE ASSOCIATION
18 Stoneybrook Close, West Bretton
Wakefield, W. Yorkshire WF4 4TP
Tel: 092485 515

NATIONAL ASSOCIATION OF BEREAVEMENT SERVICES
68 Charlton Street
London NW1 1JR
Tel: 081-388 2153
Provides a national network of support groups for the bereaved and
can put you in touch with services in your area.

NATIONAL ASSOCIATION OF VICTIM SUPPORT SCHEMES
Cranmer House, 39 Brixton Road
London SW9
Tel: 071-735 9166
Offers practical help and advice to victims of crimes. Provides
support for relatives of murder victims. Can put you in touch with
regional schemes in your area.

SANDS (STILLBIRTH AND NEONATAL DEATH SOCIETY
28 Portland Place, London W1N 3DF.
Tel: 071-436 5881
Provides a network of people bereaved in similar circumstances to
help the newly-bereaved parents of stillborn or newborn babies.

TWIN AND MULTIPLE BIRTHS ASSOCIATION
Contact: Karran Youngs
54 Parkway, Exeter
Devon EX2 9NF
Tel: 0392 431605
Runs a bereavement support group for people whose twin has died.

• Counselling

LOCAL BRANCHES OF CITIZENS' ADVICE BUREAUX can supply details
of bereavement services and counsellors in your area. Your GP can
also make referrals to counsellors or therapists. Schools, universities
and colleges often now have counselling services. Even if they are
not what you want, they can be a good starting point.

BRITISH ASSOCIATION FOR COUNSELLING
Holds lists of accredited counsellors
Tel: 0788 78328 or 78329

BRITISH ASSOCIATION OF PSYCHOTHERAPY
Tel: 081-452 9823

LONDON CLINIC OF PSYCHOANALYSIS
Tel: 071-580 4952

SOCIETY OF ANALYTICAL PSYCHOLOGY
Tel: 071-435 7696

THE WESTMINSTER PASTORAL FOUNDATION
Tel: 071-937 6956
Offers counselling throughout Great Britain

WOMEN'S THERAPY CENTRE
Tel: 071-263 6200

Index

271